I SEE WHAT YOU'RE THINKING

ANALYZE AND DECIPHER BODY LANGUAGE,
IMPROVE YOUR IMAGE, PROTECT YOURSELF,
AND FEEL CONFIDENT

THE SUCCESSFUL INTROVERTS GUIDE SERIES
BOOK 2

BRENDAN PAUL

GOLD
RIVER
PUBLISHING

The male figure on the cover was "designed by iStock."

The female figure on the cover was "designed by Freepik."

❀ Created with Vellum

INTRODUCTION

Body language is a very powerful tool. We had body language before we had speech, and apparently, 80% of what you understand in a conversation is read through the body, not the words. —Deborah Bull

"I am so happy you got the promotion!" Howard exclaimed, with a huge fake grin that didn't reach his eye, as he looked away from me. Fidgeting with his tie, he shook his head in a clear *no* (no, I am not happy!) while he kept saying *yes!*

This insight helped me to understand that Howard was hurt, as he had worked hard for the promotion *I* got, and I understood his grief. I also wasn't about to make a lifelong enemy at work.

"Well, Howard, I owe a lot of my success to you too, so what do you say we go out for an evening drink to celebrate and come up with a plan for you to nail the Anderson Account? I hear there's a huge commission associated with it."

My intuition saved my relationship with Howard, and to this day, we remain friends.

Reading Body Language—The Art of "Hearing" What's Unsaid

Want to know what the other person is thinking and feeling about you?

Who wouldn't?

Mastering the skill of reading body language can help you to do just that. Besides, you get to fine-tune your communication skills and use your body language to project more confidence, reliability, or a fun character. You can use this skill to form lasting bonds and continue a good conversation, steering clear of taboo or distressing issues, merely by picking up on signals the other person is sending. It's almost like having a crystal ball but even better because you are not stuck in a tent at the fairgrounds.

I See What You're Thinking is the second book in this very intuitive series. It's about mastering casual conversation and building relationships for introverts by being one step ahead of the game. This guide on reading body language is an exciting collection of information to help the shy introvert to decipher what's going on in the other person's head. It allows you to not only pick up all the non-verbal communication signals people send while communicating with you but also get over your own inhibitions about making casual conversation and creating the right impression with the other person.

Have you ever got up the courage to approach someone and engage in a conversation to find yourself stumped halfway through, wondering if they think you are a total social recluse or a really cool person they would like to hang out with?

If you read book one, you know there are several factors that lead to a successful conversation. One of them is forming a connection with the other person. But how do you form a connection with a total stranger, someone you just met, especially if you are stuck for words. Well, book one addresses the issue of how to formulate a successful dialog. Now let's look at the best support for deciphering the other person's reaction toward you–a hundred percent *accurate* reaction of what they are thinking—provided you successfully read all the signals and cues they are sending.

That is the guarantee I offer you in this book: exciting methods to learn the art of accurately reading body language. It's all there in the slight nod of a head, the purse of lips, the narrowing of eyes, and the direction the feet are pointing. Learn to scrutinize subtle gestures reflected through various body parts that speak the *truth* because body gestures are always an automatic reflex and, unlike words, it's hard to hide or disguise them to mean something you are not really thinking.

Here's an example of a lie that you would use:

"Yes, your pie was delicious, but I'm so full from all the delicious food, I cannot eat another bite."

Here's what you really mean:

"Oh, your pie is awful, and if I eat another bite, I may choke!"

Your words may disguise your true meaning, but your body language will give you away. You will not look directly at the person you are talking to; you will push the plate away from you, and you may blink quite a bit. Hopefully, the other person is not an expert at body language!

But then, once you become an expert at reading nonverbal cues, you become skilled at learning to hide your own nonverbal communication.

Learn the Art of Thin-Slicing Body Language

No, it's not a course taught at the local bakery!

Thin-slicing body language refers to the art of walking into a room and taking just five minutes (give or take) to quickly evaluate and get a gist of the company there. Sounds amazing? It is, and it's a technique that seems to have been invented especially for us, introverts.

You can easily become an expert at thin-slicing a room once you learn and practice the techniques of reading body language included in this book. Each chapter is carefully constructed to give a comprehensive lesson and proper understanding of how each part of the body is "talking." Remember: Every "body" speaks, and as each chapter unfolds, I will teach you the art of non-verbal communication as a step-by-step process, taking one part of the human anatomy at a time so that nothing is too complicated. Plus, you have plenty of time to practice as you progress with your reading.

A Word From the Author

I can function as an introvert's guide because I was and still am an introvert. But I learned to beat the condition. I grasped the techniques of small talk (which I have divulged in book one), how to work a room full of people, and build up my confidence even when every nuance of my body says, *turn around and run!*

I also mastered reading body language, detecting lies, and deciphering a lot about a person just from their appearance, stance, and gestures. Therefore, despite my introversion, I am able to hold my head up high, walk into a room full of strangers, assess them confidently, and use my inside information (i.e., reading body language) to successfully camouflage my insecurities to make positive connections.

I now offer *you* this same confidence and the chance to have an "edge" over your introversion by facing your biggest fears and inhibitions. If you are ready to start listening to body language, let's begin!

1

EVERY "BODY" SPEAKS

Body language and tone of voice–not words–are our most powerful assessment tools. —Christopher Voss

S ubtle movements, blinking eyes, nose touching, a rising tone of voice, etc. are all cues to a person's innermost thoughts. I like to think of them as "true thoughts" that sometimes contradict what the person is saying verbally.

Such clues serve to reveal what the other person is thinking, whether about you or the topic under discussion. Picking up on these cues is a great skill to learn as it will not only help you assess your impact on the people with whom you are engaged in conversation, but also help you fine-tune *your* conversational skills and dispel any insecurities you may have when it comes to socializing.

This chapter will introduce you to the factors governing body language. Let me start by emphasizing the importance of reading body language as more than a conversation enhancer, but rather, as a kind of hindsight given in advance to let you know what the real deal is, so you can fix, adjust or change where and what is necessary. So put on the brakes, backtrack, and avoid making statements that lead to arguments, anger, and avoidance from the other person.

What Is Body Language?

It's reading emotional reactions!

It's that initial automatic physical reaction to what the person was exposed to–be it an action, suggestion, phrase, and so on–that instigates an automatic response as a manifestation of the emotion the person felt.

Physical responses are unlike the words we speak, which are often carefully thought of and targeted to create a certain effect. They are quick and slight, so you need a sharp eye and inside knowledge to notice them and decipher the actions correctly.

Body language makes up almost 90% of our communication; shrugging shoulders, moving our limbs, pose, and tone of voice exemplify this style of non-verbal communication Yaffe (2011)

However, learning body language is not as cut and dry as you may think. It's not about deciphering how many times a person yawns when you talk about your pet hamster, for example. Or about how they keep looking at their watches as they keep talking. It's about intuition and knowing which cues and signals to trust and take note of. Without proper skills to decipher body language, we end up overreacting and making false assumptions.

Cultural Influences on Body Language

Interpreting body language requires some background knowledge.

Nodding *No*, to Mean *Yes*

Culture is one factor that dictates different body language signals. For example, in some Asian cultures, people will nod their heads in acceptance as a *yes* but in the classic *no* signal by tilting their heads from shoulder to shoulder instead of nodding forward and back. This often leaves westerners in a quandary.

Bone-Crushing Handshakes

Another one is the handshake; people in the West are taught to show strength and authority through a firm handshake. I once met a client from Texas who believed a bone-crushing handshake showed he was genuinely glad to meet me, although my poor hand certainly was not.

Conversely, in Turkey, some African countries, and the East, that gesture is perceived as arrogant and pushy, and therefore a gentle, limp handshake or bow of the head is appropriate. My Texan friend would disagree, but perhaps I can introduce him to the bow and save myself some pain.

Signaling *OK* and Insulting Someone

The *ok* gesture you make with your thumb and forefinger curved into an O can be very insulting when you are visiting countries like Brazil, Greece or Spain. It literally means you are calling that person an a-hole (oops). This is one for your travel notes and to never use if you want to avoid being chased by an angry mob.

The Controversial *Come Here* Gesture

Even the simple gesture of *come here* used in the US to call someone over, where you fold four fingers down on an upturned palm and use the index finger to beckon, is thought to be very rude in China and several East Asian nations. The gesture is used to call dogs. Again, these are valuable travel tips to avoid being chased by an angry mob.

Looking Them in the Eye

Eye contact too can have different meanings. In the West, we believe strong eye contact is a sign of sincerity and strength. But in some East Asian nations and the Middle East, eye contact is considered arrogant and rude.

Well, then how *do* we read body language without offending or getting offended?

The general norm is that similar body language signals exist between similar cultures and communities. Therefore, you can safely read body language between communities you live in. Hence, this book looks at universal body language gestures akin to the US and western countries.

For times when you are traveling outside of your country or community, it's best to read up about cultural differences and body language signals pertaining to the destination.

Why Is Body Language Important?

Why can't you use words to effectively communicate? What's the hype about body language?

Here are the benefits of reading body language.

It's a Fail-Safe Lie Detector

Body language is almost always an automatic response— and also a pretty good lie detector for people who can read physical gestures accurately. Also, let's not forget that physical appearances are what we judge before analyzing words.

For example, no matter how vigorously the other person is nodding their head in agreement to your never-ending tale about how you caught a giant catfish on an eight-hour fishing trip, their body language (looking around the room, over your shoulder, etc.) will tell you they are looking around for a lifeline —an excuse to get away.

It Helps to Gauge the Success of a Conversation

Subtle signs, such as looking over your shoulder, fidgeting, and allowing their eyes to wander around the room (while still nodding to what you are saying) suggest you are having a one-sided discussion with someone who has tuned you out.

Sometimes, the other person may fold their arms across their chest to say, *I don't agree,* although outwardly they are using words to say *yes, I see.* Reading these subtle signals is a good heads-up for when you are discussing a sensitive subject or putting across a point of view.

Sometimes the person you are conversing with may say nothing at all. Instead, they will stand with their arms folded across their chest, eyes slit, and their head tilted to a side—indicating they are reaching boiling point. Take it as a sign to change the course of the conversation before it turns into a full-scale argument.

Let's say you're at an important interview; you can assume it's going well if you and the interviewer are looking each other in the eye, and they listen intently to what you are saying. Leaning toward you, smiling, and showing interest are additional signs of a successful interview. However, if eye contact is avoided between both parties, it's a good sign the interview has not reached an amicable platform, and you are not making an impressive impact.

It Influences Important Decisions

Let's continue with the interview scenario.

Your body language can influence important decisions—whether you get the job or that coveted promotion. Your *stance* can project more about you. Good body language skills can work in your favor because a larger percentage of your character will be evaluated via your physical gestures. Most interviewers look for these hidden signals to evaluate a person, which means your stance can make or break a deal.

Posture, facial expressions, and eye contact can enhance your chances of success or sabotage them. Quite often, first impressions are formed by analyzing physical appearances, and you will be viewed as aggressive, trustworthy, submissive, attractive, or even suspicious, based on facial and body language signals you generate. All it takes is one tenth of a second for someone to make an assumption about you based on your body language. Your first impression (Willis & Todorov, 2006).

It Reveals Visual Dominance When It Comes to Decision-Making

Visual impressions dominate decisions. It's a universally accepted phenomenon and also a survival mode that has kept us, humans, safe over time—we see a predator, we run away and take cover!

The theory has been put to the test and proven. Bias toward vision as a primary decision-making tool has been attributed to the fact that we place importance on what we see above all else —seeing is believing, as the old adage goes (Hutmacher, 2019).

How to Use Body Language Successfully

Based on the above theory, you can learn to project successful physical gestures. Here are some tips to keep in mind whether you are trying to impress a panel of interviewers or join a conversation at a social event.

- Project the right attitude: Stand looking aloof with a don't-care attitude at a party, and you can expect people to avoid you like the plague. Adjusting your attitude to suit the situation will yield successful results. Sit in at interviews with an aura of excitement, confidence, and openness to learning, and you can give off positive vibes.
- Make eye contact: Eye contact showcases sincerity and openness, drawing people toward you. Be sure to keep it simple, avoiding a psychotic lock of eyes. A good method of making effective eye contact is to try and determine the color of the other person's eyes— do so subtly without peering into their face and infringing on their personal space.
- Smile: This is the universal gesture that says I am friendly and approachable. Again, avoid the maniac style grin that says run away before I stuff you in a sack. If smiling is hard for you, practice a subtle

smile in the mirror before you attend a big event. As introverts, we often wait for the other person to smile first but break that rule and enjoy the results —always smile first.

- Lean in but not too much: Show you are engaged in the conversation and interested by slightly leaning in but do avoid getting too close. A distance of two feet is a good rule of thumb to maintain.
- Gestures: Do you use your hands, eyes, and head to indicate how passionate you are about what you are discussing? If you do, chances are you will be perceived as energetic, warm, and pleasant by the other person. People who are more composed and use fewer bodily gestures to express themselves will often be perceived as more analytical, logical, and more practical than passionate.

There is such a thing as over-gesturing. This happens when you go overboard with hand gestures. Raising hands and arms above your head in a bid to impress can be seen negatively, being interpreted as weak or trying too hard and therefore, less believable.

Mehrabian's Communication Module

At this juncture of our analysis of body language, it's important to look at Dr. Albert Mehrabian's theory. The psychologist theorized that only 7% of communication is verbal as the rest is delivered through body language and tone of voice. This would be true if, for example, you think back to a text message you received from someone which you interpreted to be rude when that was not the message the other person was delivering. Attribute those misunderstandings to a lack of physical deciphering or, in other words, not *seeing* the person to read their body language and thus gauge the emotion attached to the message.

While the Mehrabian's module is often quoted as attributing 7% to verbal communication and 93% to non-verbal communication, it is only the gist of the module presented and is not an accurate quote of the psychiatrist's study done in 1967.

Positive and Negative Body Language as Discovered by Mehrabian

In his study *Inference Attitudes from Non-Verbal Communication in Two Channels,* Mehrabian categorized people's non-verbal attitudes as:

- positive
- negative
- neutral

His study centered on three factors: the tone of voice, words used, and facial expressions. Through the study of these three factors, the psychiatrist aimed to pinpoint which had the most impact on the listener–was it words or actions that spoke the loudest?

The conclusion was words had the lowest significance. Feelings and emotions were best expressed accurately via facial expressions, which were enhanced and confirmed through tone of voice (Mehrabian and Ferris).

What Happens When Actions Don't Match Words?

How often have you listened to someone thinking *okay, he is hiding something.* You probably got that vibe because the speaker's words did not match his actions.

Mehrabian's module covers this conundrum too and goes on to conclude that when inconsistencies exist between actions and words, people naturally tend to believe non-verbal communication.

He said he liked my cooking, but I just knew he disliked it!

The same applies to the tone of voice when it does not match the words used. For example, using a negative word with a positive tone will diminish the threat the word holds.

"Get lost you little rascals!" she scolded in a light tone which told the children that mom was not really angry.

Therefore, it was concluded that when combined with actions, factors such as negative and positive tonality changed the way words were interpreted.

Based on that theory, Mehrabian created the following formula: Emotion and attitude communicated verbally were 7% + Tonality communicated 38% + Facial expressions 55% = 100%

Points to Consider from Mehrabian's Module

Here's how to successfully test the theory:

- During a phone conversation you cannot communicate via facial expressions. Hence, while choosing your words carefully, the tone you speak them in will have a bigger impact.

"I called to ask you to come in to work tomorrow, I know it's a Saturday but..."

The above statement, when said over the phone, can sound demanding and aggressive, or necessary and apologetic at the same time. It all depends on the tone of voice you use.

- In emails or texts, emoticons can come to the rescue. Word choice is important, but to make up for the lack of facial expressions and tonality, choose emoticons to represent your facial expressions and to make sure your message is conveyed in the right sense. Just make sure you choose the right emoticon before you hit send.

- When conveying bad news, choose a face-to-face confrontation instead of relying on an email or phone call. Let's say you need to give a colleague some negative feedback. You will successfully convey the message, without causing offense, during a personal conversation. Use the same opportunity to gauge the other person's reaction to the message so you may tone down or change your choice of words to lessen the impact of the bad news you are delivering.

Tip: Study a Person's Baseline Body Language

A good tip for reading body language among people you know is to study their baseline cues. What are their normal non-verbal signals? Do they gesture with their arms a lot, look you in the eye, touch your shoulder, etc.? Studying baseline body language helps to pick up the moment something is off. All you do is look for non-verbal cues that are out of the ordinary.

UNDERSTANDING Negative and Positive Body Language

Here are examples to decipher negative and positive body language, which will make it easier for you to identify strong emotions and thoughts the other person is experiencing.

NEGATIVE BODY LANGUAGE

1. Distress, Unhappiness, and Disagreement

A person who is bored and distracted during a conversation, or unhappy and disagreeing with what's being said, will display the following traits.

- A lack of facial expressions. All you get is a blank stare that displays little or no emotional response to what you're saying. They look tense and sometimes as though they want to run away to another corner of the room. This is true if the talker is self-obsessed or utterly boring. You may have experienced the run-away emotion from time to time, but did you know your face can display that emotion?
- Folding their arms across their chest as a sort of barricade. They are protesting or disagreeing with what's being said.
- Eyes that look down avoiding any type of connection with yours, signal unhappiness or disagreement.

These cues are red flags to let you know that it's time to show some empathy, tone down what you are saying, and become more sensitive to the listener's emotions.

Focus on easing their tension by choosing positive words.

Here's an example of how you can use reading negative body language (point 1) to ease a situation (point 2)

Point 1: "If only you had paid more attention to the rising numbers, we may have been able to sell the stocks in time."

Save face and ease tension with this follow-up comment.

Point 2: "But then again, there is no guarantee that selling the stocks would have made a killer profit, so I guess the damage is minimal."

2. Boredom

- Looking over your shoulder as you speak, turning your head to see what others are doing, or gazing

into the distance are all signs the listener is bored or preoccupied.
- Sitting with shoulders slumped and head bent. Are they snoozing while you talk? Maybe not, but they certainly are not interested in what you are saying.
- Distracting themselves with other tasks while you talk, fidgeting with an object, drawing doodles, tapping their fingers in impatience, turning their phones on and off, and so on.

When you notice these signs, turn the conversation around; ask the other person a personal question. Something that gets them talking about themselves. Show interest and listen attentively, using the information to probe further and ask appropriate questions.

3. Anxiety, Nervousness, and Tension

People's inner fears and emotional distress can sometimes be displayed through their actions if the conversation is making them nervous, evokes unpleasant memories, or has gone beyond their comfort zone.

- Blinking eyes several times can indicate nervousness or lack of self-confidence.
- Biting nails indicates stress, uncertainty, and insecurity.
- Locking ankles is indicative of stressful thoughts and anxiety.

Pay close attention to the signals the other person is sending, and you will be able to identify factors in the conversation that are making them uncomfortable. You can then steer the conversation toward a more positive angle.

Positive Body Language

Spotting positive body language in the other person is very

reassuring as it will uplift your confidence and conversational skills. Positive signals will confirm the person is engaged and displays interest, excitement, happiness, and trust. Noticing these cues will make *you* feel at ease, comfortable, and liked.

How Can I Display Positive Body Language?

The vibe you give off is important to make a good first impression; you must appear confident, genuine, and relaxed when conversing. In other words, you need to project a positive self-image.

Here are some tips:

- Avoid the resting bitch face and smile—it's a universal icebreaker. A warm smile is reassuring and highly infectious. If you look grouchy (you have what is called a *resting bitch face),* people will avoid you, even though you feel conversational inside. Therefore, don't wait for the other person to smile first; go ahead and smile.

What's a resting bitch face (RBF)?

As explained in book one, RBF is an unintentional expression that takes over a person's face when they are in repose. Unknowingly, they look cross because their faces naturally take on an angry/grumpy look. Get online and look up a few celebrities identified with RBF, and you will understand.

- Have a relaxed stance. Whether sitting or standing, don't slouch. Sit or stand upright. Don't stand with your hands on your hips, it can be interpreted as aggressive. Instead, have your hands by your side. Lean in slightly to show you are interested in what they are saying, not too much, and maintain personal space. Use an open-body posture. Do not fold your arms, or cross your legs, as they can look like barriers.

- Don't touch your face, fiddle with your hair, or listen/talk with your palm or fingers covering your mouth. They are signals that are often interpreted as dishonest, especially if you are answering someone's questions.

- Show interest. Let the other person know that their conversation is engaging. Rubbing your chin or touching your face in a thinking gesture is allowed because it shows you are trying to comprehend what's being said—as perhaps when discussing a complex topic. Ask questions, though, instead of nodding your head in agreement to every word, when you don't understand a thing that's being said. Asking for clarification or elaboration helps you to learn more about the subject.

- Use open-hand communication. This is especially important when you are making a presentation or speech. Using such gestures as extending your arm and having your palms open when talking to people says you are open to suggestions and a two-way discussion.

While the above tips are food for thought, you can fine-tune your body language reading and projecting skills by learning about each part of your anatomy and the role they play when it comes to non-verbal communication.

And because the human body contains several parts that we use to *talk with*, let's break it down. The next chapter will take you through your lower body gestures. Understanding the subtle cues they provide–from hands on the hips to the direction the feet are pointing, for instance–is very exciting and interesting.

2

LANGUAGE OF THE LOWER BODY

Language is a more recent technology. Your body language, your eyes, your energy will come through to your audience before you even start speaking. —Peter Guber

Feet can talk as well as they walk!

Did you know that your lower body has quite the vocabulary and speaks a lot about your personality, thoughts, and emotions?

Non-verbal communication through your legs and feet can shine a negative or positive light on you, even influencing the outcome of certain events.

Let me tell you a little story.

I once conducted a set of interviews for a Japanese client who was looking for a personal assistant to work at their US office. After shortlisting the candidates to two people, James and Andrew were called in for a final interview at which my client, Mr. Osaka, sat in. He insisted on placing the interviewee's chairs at a distance of about four feet from where we were seated and called in the two men for a joint discussion.

Both candidates arrived on time, and after the preliminary introductions sat down in their strategically placed chairs in front of us. Mr. Osaka began with a narration of the history of his company. I noticed he kept his gaze on the two men and was observant of their behavior as he spoke. Once done with his explanation, he discreetly circled Andrew's name but continued with a thorough Q&A session with both men. Satisfied, he thanked them and ended the interview with a promise of a call by afternoon to let them know the outcome.

As soon as they left, Osaka turned to me and said, "Hire Andrew."

Curious, I asked him how he chose Andrew before he even began the proper Q&A session, as I noticed him circle the young man's name at the beginning of the discussion.

Osaka replied: "His feet told me he was interested in the history of my company, as they were pointed directly at me and placed together. James sat and turned his feet pointed sideways as I began to speak, displaying disinterest. These were the first non-verbal signs that gave me a heads up about who was the right choice for my company."

Andrew is still working for Osaka, in the capacity of CEO, and is a loved and dedicated employee of the company.

The Language of Feet—Dirty Dancing or Ballet?

You could be wearing flip-flops or knee-high boots, but that won't stop your feet from talking and revealing too much about your personality—not to someone who understands body language, anyway.

Body language experts regard feet as the most revealing and often forgotten form of non-verbal communication that conveys a lot about an individual or a group of people.

Feet disclose your feelings, your level of interest, and even your attraction toward someone. Their impact is so important that in some cultures there are rules to how you "handle" your feet.

For example, in most Southeast Asian nations, feet that point at a person, are propped higher than someone's shoulder level, or placed, rather leisurely, on a desk, etc. are considered rude and arrogant gestures. So, you see how easily a simple physical gesture, one you would otherwise consider a relaxed pose, can cause offense to someone else.

The First Rule of Thumb When Reading Body Language: Understanding Circumstances

Howard was in a rush. He was late for an important meeting and arrived at the venue five minutes late. In the lobby of the building, he met Susan, an old friend from college. Susan was delighted to meet Howard and started a conversation that recapped their past. But as she spoke, she noticed Howard looked agitated, and his body language said he wanted to leave. His feet were pointed away from Susan in an almost "I need to flee" gesture.

Insulted, Susan said a hasty goodbye and left with a frown on her face. Howard was, of course, happy to see her and made a mental note to call her and schedule a meet-up.

In this scenario, while Susan read Howard's body language correctly, she misunderstood the circumstance (or context) behind the behavior and, therefore, left with a bad impression of her old friend.

In order to avoid misunderstanding body language, it's important to try and discover the true circumstance leading to a person's behavior so that you make an accurate reading of body language to understand what's unsaid and why.

Well then, how do you find out the true circumstance behind a person's body language when you don't possess a crystal ball or weird psychic powers?

The answer is lip compression.

What Is Lip Compression?

To understand the true circumstance behind a person's body language, we need to be observant and analytical. Our lips are the most exposed body part when it comes to non-verbal communication. They are, in fact, the first physical indication of our emotions.

How many times have you noticed a person compress their lips when you requested them to do something you know they would rather avoid?

"Caleb, let's work over the weekend and finish this project."

"Ok," Caleb replied through compressed lips.

What does this mean, a positive statement (Okay) with negative body language?

The answer here depends on the circumstance. Why is Caleb unhappy with working over the weekend, although he agrees to do so?

Using Lip Compression to Understand Circumstance

Before you become judgmental by reading a person's body language, you need to understand the circumstance influencing those body language skills.

Here are the most common reasons.

- A person is feeling uncomfortable; a classic cue is smiling, rather oddly, through compressed lips.
- You just told them something they would rather not talk about and don't want to proceed further.
- They are feeling embarrassed, shy, or ashamed and don't wish to talk about the issue.

Use these cues in conjunction with other body language signals to come to an accurate assessment of the other person's emotional message.

Feet—Interpreting Their Poses

Time for some footy fun. Study the following poses and see how many you decipher accurately as you go about your daily interactions. Remember, practice makes perfect, so remain observant at all times.

1. Territory-claiming pose—standing with feet apart and hands on hips

This is a power pose that is used to show dominance. You will notice it among people of authority–the policeman who pulls you over for speeding, a sergeant addressing a fresh intake of cadets, and so on. If anyone pulls this pose, it's a clear indication they are trying to wield authority or power.

1. Attraction—feet that point toward you

A person who stands with their feet pointed toward you is subconsciously indicating they are at ease in your company.

Feet that are directed at you when conversing with someone is a positive signal to indicate they are engaged and interested in what you are saying. It can also mean they are attracted to you. But hold on before you splurge on the chocolates and flowers. Do not rush to a conclusion; instead, tie up the feet cue with other signals to be one hundred percent sure it's attraction.

Tip: A good cue for men to gauge if a woman is interested and flirting with them is a common gesture where the woman slips her shoe off from the back of her foot and swings it against her heel. But watch out if she suddenly slips the shoe back onto her foot, as it means you said something that made her uncomfortable!

1. Disinterested—feet that point away

If a person you are conversing with has their feet pointed away from you, it could mean they are not interested in what you say and are looking for an exit route. Again, hold on before you stomp off in a huff. Don't forget the "understanding circumstance" rule where you need to gauge the context of the situation. Maybe the other person is in a rush, needs to catch someone else before they leave regarding an important matter, etc.

1. Authority, dominance, and comfort—crossed feet

If someone stretches out their legs and crosses their feet, it could have several meanings. You will be able to gauge the correct one, given the situation.

Here's what crossed feet can mean.

- Dominance—the person is establishing their authoritative position of power.
- Anxiety—they are nervous about the situation/discussion and feel uncomfortable and exposed.
- Comfort—feet stretched out could also mean the person is feeling extremely comfortable in your company. Such poses are common among friends.

Feet Position in a Group
Sometimes we feel uncomfortable chatting with a group of people. We feel self-conscious or that we are not interesting enough to hold the attention of everyone. A good way to overcome these inhibitions and learn more about how interesting you are is to observe the feet in a group of people you are having a conversation with.

If you and another person are talking in a group, check to see in which direction the listeners' feet are pointing. If they are pointing to you, then you are regarded as the main interest. If they are pointed at someone else, then they hold the majority's interest.

Again, keep in mind that circumstance matters here. The person who most people are pointing their feet at may hold a seniority advantage. They may be of vital importance to the other's goals, or to someone who garners respect based on their position of power at home or the workplace.

When Feet Dance

I don't mean the cha-cha or rumba, but rather, the restless feet that can't stop moving even when the person is speaking or listening to a conversation. This type of cue is an excellent example of how your *limbic brain* controls your body language.

While experts confirm that body language can be trained to be used to your advantage, and that is what I aim to teach you, feet remain the most sensitive to emotional displays. Therefore, the movement and placement of feet, when deciphered correctly, will give you an insight into what the other person is trying to say, thus making you privy to their feelings. Then you will be able to assess if they are feeling aggressive, confident, or telling the truth. Therefore, it becomes important to watch a person's feet while conversing with them if you want to read body language accurately.

What's Your Limbic Brain?

It's part of what's called the reptilian brain, the most primal section of your brain which controls essential functions, such as your heart rate, and body temperature, as well as regulating your breathing. Part of your limbic brain is the amygdala and hippocampus.

The amygdala is responsible for stimulating your fight-or-flight mode, alerting you to danger, and instigating survival behavior such as fear, aggression, or retreat in reaction to a threat (Baxter & Croxson, 2012).

The hippocampus performs several vital tasks, among them the control of your mood, feelings of pleasure, pain, sex drive, and so on; such emotions will be displayed through body language (Dhikav & Anand, 2012).

Since feet are the most sensitive to your limbic brain, they become the most accurate and detailed tool for you to read body language.

Happiness, Excitement, and Anticipation Displayed Through Bouncy Feet

Bouncy feet indicate any one of the above emotions, whether a person is seated or standing. Hearing good news, receiving a gift, or standing in line will evoke the gesture to signify happiness, anticipation, or excitement. Children are good examples of displaying bouncy happy feet.

Feet That Go Into Hiding

If the person you are talking to suddenly starts shuffling their feet, or they retract their feet so much that you hardly see them, it could mean the topic of the conversation is making them uncomfortable. Thus, they either want to leave or change the course of the discussion.

The Stomper

Foot-stopping is usually reserved for children. Kids are quite free at stomping their feet when they are angry, stressed, and unhappy. It's a powerful gesture that gives a direct message, so adults tend to shy away from such an open display of emotion. However, it does happen and can indicate anger in dire circumstances as well as moments when a sudden epiphany occurs.

The Tapper

We all indulge in this gesture now and then. Tapping feet takes place when the ball of the heel remains on the floor, and you tap the front potion, often in rhythm to the music you are enjoying. This indicates a relaxed and happy mood.

Strike a Pose

A person's posture is greatly influenced by the stance their legs and feet take. And from what we have learned so far, feet do not lie. So, let's get this right and start reading those poses accurately.

One Foot Forward to Close the Gap

A person standing with one foot forward is literally saying, "I want to get closer to you,'" signaling attraction. It could also mean they are wholly interested in what you are saying. Therefore, make sure to understand the context of the situation before you misinterpret interest for romance. Either way, this foot stance is a positive signal.

The V Shape That Welcomes

So, you are chatting to your crush, and you look down, and bam, they have their feet in a V shape, and you are within that V. Make the most of the opportunity because a V-shaped foot stance pointing toward you shows interest. Ask them for a date, or hint toward one, and chances are you will be successful.

Standing at Attention

This may have been your standard pose when you were talking to your teacher in grade school. It's also a common stance for military people when addressing a superior. The smart pose is where you stand with a straight posture and feet placed together.

This type of parallel pose indicates uncertainty. People who are not sure about their position, such as students or cadets in the military, adopt this pose. Think about it, the position with a ramrod stance and feet together represents a bowling pin, and one good shove will tip the person over—hence it's indicative of vulnerability or a lack of certainty.

Standing Your Ground With Feet Apart

Conversely to the parallel pose, someone who stands with their feet apart is indicating dominance. A typical male pose; although I do know many females too who adopt the stance, this one is similar to the wonder woman pose, and reflects power. Go ahead and change your parallel pose to a power pose whenever you feel defeated and need a confidence boost.

Think of the cowboys in those old westerns you watched, with their legs apart and thumbs hooked into their belt loops, staring with slitted eyes to see who dares draw their gun first. It's a powerful and intimidating pose.

Crossed Legs or Arms

This one, too, is probably a common pose you or others adopt, during a meeting or get-together, when feeling nervous, exposed, and unsure.

Standing cross-legged, often away from other people, signals uncertainty, being often seen at meetings where not everyone is familiar with each other. It's a protective and a guarding-of-privacy pose. For example, standing crossed-legged in a typical scissor pose suggests one's covering and guarding their weakest area, the genitals. It doesn't get any more graphic than that.

A man or woman standing with their legs crossed is sending a positive yet mixed message—they are staying, but they are also guarding themselves. These are subconscious reactions that come through our body language and are a good gauge for assessing a person's vulnerabilities.

Icebreaker poses

If you really want to put your body language reading skills to the test, go ahead and test some of the theories. A good example is to observe people meeting for the first time. You will notice how they go from the crossed-legged defensive pose to the open-palm, foot-forward, relaxed pose, the more they chat and get to know each other.

Observe, and you will notice how the stances take the following order.

Meeting for the first time:

- Arms folded; legs crossed in a defensive mode

As the chat continues:

- Arms will come down, and the palm may be open and turned toward the other person on and off.
- Legs uncross.
- One foot may move forward as they become more familiar with each other, or the feet are pointed at each other.
- Arms may get folded across the chest, but this time it's not a tight pose and is more out of habit than as a defensive pose. This arm cross takes place with one arm placed over the other, instead of becoming a tight crossed arm pose with the palms tucked under, indicating a defense mechanism has been activated.

The Figure-Four Pose

This pose makes the person look like a number four (4) as they sit with one leg bent at the knee, raised to let the ankle of that leg rest on the knee of the other leg. The arm on the side of the bent leg rests along the length of the crossed leg, the elbow placed on the knee, as they slouch forward. It's not the classic cross, but an open-leg cross that looks like this— a 4.

The pose is often used by males, although women too use it, maybe not in front of men if they do not want to appear masculine. The pose is indicative of an argumentative or strong character. Men who adopt the pose are perceived as powerful and dominant. It's more common in the US and less in European nations, while in some cultures, such as southeast Asia and the Middle East, this pose will be considered an insult since it shows the soles of the person's foot or shoe on the raised leg—precisely where dirt gathers.

The Nervous Pose

This is a very feminine pose when one ankle is wrapped around the other with the length of one leg pressed against the back of the other. Women feeling nervous will often adopt this pose. Men on a date, when noticing this pose, can initiate some relaxing moves that will put their date at ease.

Sitting With Legs Entwined

This, too, is similar to standing with entwined legs, being indicative of a nervous disposition. This mostly feminine pose can be misinterpreted as it's also adopted by women prone to wearing short skirts–the pose creates a barrier and allows the person to sit without revealing too much. Women who often adopt this pose in short skirts will continue to do so even in pants, sending the wrong signal. Therefore, check the context of the situation before you make any judgments. Are they merely trying to sit without revealing too much, or are they nervous?

The Parallel Sitting Pose

This one, too, is more related to females since it's physically possible for them to do so. Sitting parallel means to sit with both legs pressed against each other as you would when standing at attention—men cannot do so when seated. It's an exclusive feminine pose that most men vote as attractive.

Attracted or Not!

This last pose is for all people confused about signals they are receiving from someone they admire.

A classic pose where the male is trying to attract someone is when they stand with legs apart, arms held in a wide pose, and a foot pointing toward the other person. A classic courtship ritual from the animal kingdom, standing with their legs apart, reveals a man's groin area while extending their arms, perhaps by hooking their thumbs in their belt loop to extend the elbows, creating a larger illusion of their torso. (Think about peacocks who puff out their tails to attract the peahen, or the gorilla beating his chest.) While people don't get that graphic, our body language subtly displays similar cues.

But are those feelings reciprocated?

Let's say a woman is receiving the signals mentioned above but is not interested–what will she do?

She will turn her body away from the man, trying to look as inconsequential as possible by folding her arms together. It is also a pose to say, "I am not interested." Look at her feet: they will be pointing away, while her legs are placed together in a *nope, you're not impressing me*, gesture. (No open V position here)

What's Hip About Hips?

Do you know the song about hips not lying? Well, there's more to that verse than a mere catchy tune because hips speak loads, and you are going to learn to listen to them. What's more, you can learn to *control* your hips to convey non-verbal messages and give yourself a confidence boost.

Hands-on-Hips Pose

Sandra was a college swimmer; she was one of the best in her class, yet she suffered nervous tendencies whenever she stood at the starting block. Her coach, noticing her weakness, gave her some advice. "Use a power pose to gain confidence," he told her.

At her next race, Sandra stood at the block and noticed the same pre-race jitters returning. She consciously shifted her pose; she stood with spread legs, looked straight ahead, *and* moved her hands to her hips. She stood like Wonder Woman, ready to battle an enemy, and suddenly her demeanor changed; she felt a surge of energy and confidence and climbed the starter block with more determination than she had before.

This is one example of how you can use your hips to talk to yourself: to invoke confidence and build self-esteem. However, hands on hips can have several different meanings.

Commanding Attention

"Daniel, you cannot have cookies before lunch, and that's

final!" Laura reiterated with her hands on her hips as she tried to discipline her angry toddler.

Hands-on-hips are often used by people who want to gain attention to themselves; people who demand they are taken note of. Such power poses can be seen not only among angry moms but even a manager giving a speech to their team will want to exert authority with the hands-on hip pose. Your favorite football player who confronts the referee for what he feels is an unfair judgment will have his hands on his hips, with elbows jutting out to make him look bigger, aggressive, and demanding.

The hands-on-hips command attention in non-aggressive situations too. A woman who wants to show off her clothes will pose with hands on her hips to say, "look at me," thus calling attention to herself. Runway models often walk with this pose to draw attention to the clothes they are modeling.

The Power Pose

The Wonder Woman or Superman pose is adopted when people want to appear aggressive or exert influence. It's almost like marking their territory.

This pose can be highly influential when you need a confidence boost. Most introverts often try to downplay their actions, but adopting this pose can give you an immense boost of self-confidence.

Research confirms that power poses work. They are capable of increasing testosterone levels, improving tolerance, enhancing feelings of power, and decreasing levels of cortisol, the stress hormone (Carney et al. 2010). It's the perfect elixir for when you feel too much like an introvert and need some courage.

Single Hand on Hip

"Frank, where do you think you are going?"

Margret asked her spouse, one hand on her hip, as he tried to slip out of the house unnoticed. Poor Frank was not fast enough and ended up helping his spouse spring-clean the house when all he wanted to do was meet the boys for a drink. However, Frank recognized the ultimatum in that one-hand-on-the-hip pose and decided it was in his best interest to stay and help.

If someone uses this pose with you, it could mean you have either irritated them or have pushed too many buttons, and they are now giving you an ultimatum to stop talking or face the consequences. Conversely, you will find this pose works to your benefit, too, when you use it, especially if you are a parent.

However, for this pose, too, circumstance matters. Make a judgment call, especially if there is no reason for someone to want to get aggressive with you. In this case, they could be using the pose as a familiar way of relaxing. Watch a few videos of celebrities on the red carpet, and you will notice most women pose with one hand on their hips– a relaxing gesture that means they are *not* asking you to go clean your room. Remember: For all body language, circumstance matters.

The Inquisitive Pose—Hands on Hip, Thumbs Pointing Down

You will notice the Superman or Wonder Woman pose is held with the hands-on-hips and thumbs pointing backward. However, if you notice someone standing with their hands on their hips and thumbs pointing down, it could signal curiosity.

Classic examples of when you can observe this pose are perhaps when there is an incident taking place in public, such as a fight, a car accident, or even when someone stands up to put forward a question at a forum.

Tip for manipulating this pose in your favor: Whenever you find yourself using the power pose in an aggressive situation where you are angry, argumentative, etc., and find yourself standing with your hands on your hips, thumbs pointing back, make a conscious effort and shift your thumbs to point down. This simple gesture will turn your aggression into curiosity, and you can become more tolerant to try and understand the situation rather than trying to steamroll your way through.

Hips That Are Meant to Be Together

The phrase *they were joined at the hips, and very much in love* is pretty close to the truth. Distance between the hips of two people can tell you a lot. Let's say you met someone at a get-together and thought you really hit it off, but when it was time for a farewell hug, you noticed them keeping their hips as far away from you as they could. What does that mean?

Sadly, it means the other person does not feel as close to you as you do to them. However, if you are lucky and someone comes in for a giant hug squishing their hips against yours, it's a sure sign of mutual attraction—unless *you* decide to keep a hip distance.

The closeness of hips can be judged without involving a hug. If you want to gauge the level of attraction between you and someone else, check for the closeness of hips as you talk or stand close to each other. Keeping a distance of over one foot is a negative sign that you are probably not hitting it off with each other.

The Humble Hip

Using the hips to bow is a classic signal for extending respect and modesty. The Japanese call the gesture *ojigi,* and it consists of a deep bow bent at the hips—not the waist–to signify respect. As such, the gesture is effective when you need to display unpretentiousness to garner trust, as you appear less aggressive and more humble.

It is this show of humility and respect that makes actors take a deep bow at the end of the show; the wider the applause and appreciation, the deeper the bow, which says, *thank you from the bottom of my heart.*

If you don't want to appear too eccentric, you can use the bow as a simple nod of the head, where you bend your head forward and perhaps take off any headgear as a mark of respect. This is non-verbal communication at its best and will earn you respect as you extend the same.

Hips That Shift

Have you ever noticed how a person adjusts themselves while seated and engaged in conversation by moving their hips? The gesture can be a cue for one of the following reasons.

- There is no hidden meaning, and the person is merely settling in to get more comfy. You can assume this as the reason for the hip shift if you are both enjoying an amicable conversation with no other body language to highlight discomfort.
- They are feeling nervous, embarrassed, or uncomfortable. If the hip shift occurs with a sudden avoidance of eye contact, biting their nails, and other signals of nervousness, it's a good indication the other person is experiencing some difficulty with what's been discussed.
- The person is taking a breather. This type of hip shift will happen if you are locked in an argument with someone, and they feel they need to reassess their stance. The hip shift will take place as a type of reboot that gives them a new perspective or a breather to continue with the argument, debate, and so on.
- They are bored. If you are locked in a conversation with someone who keeps looking over your shoulder, looks distracted, and keeps shifting their hips, it's a cue to say, *I'm bored, and I need to get away!*

As you can see, you need to judge the circumstance during which the hip shift takes place to make an accurate judgment of this non-verbal cue.

The Wiggly Hip

Do you often find yourself swaying your hips, moving them up and down, or side-to-side when you feel impatient or bored, such as when standing in line? It's an automatic self-soothing gesture that resembles the rocking motion someone uses to soothe a baby, almost as if you are telling yourself to remain calm and be patient—*this endless line is going to move fast.*

If you are chatting to a person who suddenly starts swaying their hips, but not in rhythm to any music that's being played, chances are you're boring the pants off them. Therefore, wind up and end the conversation. Conversely, pay attention to your body language and avoid any hip swaying if you don't want to offend the person you're talking to, such as your boss, who's rambling on about his new car.

Hands-On Hips, and Thumbs Tucked Into the Belt or Waist

This one is a typical cowboy pose that generally reeks of courtship or, rather, a man trying to draw attention to his, ahem, crown jewels.

Standing with hands on hips and thumbs tucked into the belt or top of the pants is a pose mostly adopted by men, who are probably trying to look attractive to a female in the group.

If you see this pose being adopted, observe, and spot the female the attention is directed at. Of course, there are some women who use this pose too, but merely as a power pose, not to attract men. This stance can also be intimidating at times; thus, if you are in a group where someone else considers themselves the more powerful individual, your belt-buckle-thumb-hook pose can look like an act of aggression.

The best way to use the pose is to send a flirty message and let the other person know you are interested.

Swaying Hip Walk

While men stand around with their thumbs tucked into their belt buckles, women will amp up the heat with a sexy hip-swaying walk so sultry that Marilyn Monroe is given credit for fine-tuning the stride.

The *Monroe Walk,* as some like to call it, is a wonderful swaying walk that makes a woman's gait look like a pendulum that's swinging from side to side. It's often used as a sign to say the female is trying to attract your attention. And so, if you are out on a date with a lady who decides to walk away from you with a full swing to her hips, chances are she is hoping to attract you. Just don't stare too hard!

Covering Your Vitals—The Fig Leaf Pose

Watch people on stage waiting their turn to give a speech, and you will see them standing as though they are naked statues desperately trying to cover their exposed groin area. The hands resemble the fig leaf, and some statues are coyly used as a cover-up, hence the name.

This stance, where the arms cross the hips to spread the hands across the groin area, signals vulnerability, as when someone is on a stage in front of an audience, or attending a party where they don't know the people, which makes them feel exposed. Seeing someone use this pose is your cue to help them feel more at ease.

Using Your Hips to Dance Sexy

This one is for the ladies. If you don't possess killer dance moves, you can still look attractive while dancing with some good hip-swaying moves. Send the signal across the dance floor that you are ready to *party* with some simple yet sexy moves that involve your hips. Dancers with greater hip swings and asymmetric arm and thigh movements were voted as having the most attractive moves on the dance floor. While hip swaying works for women, a firm hand grip works to increase attraction for men (McCarty et al., 2017). So, go ahead, grab your partner by the hand, as firmly as you can, and sway them across the dance floor!

Hips don't lie, and feet are the most accurate and sensitive to non-verbal communication. But remember that practice makes perfect. Fine-tune your lower body reading skills, making sure to gauge the circumstance or context of the situation before making a judgment.

And so, since you cannot go around looking at the lower torso of people all the time, let's move on to reading the upper body because there is a whole new language to be learned there.

3

LANGUAGE OF THE UPPER BODY

It's spoken with a shoulder shrug, a side-to-side of the head, and roll of the eyes. It means: "I can't even fathom your reality, but I've decided to just accept it and move on." —Kevin Hart

Shoulders speak volumes, telling you if the person is tired, dejected, or proud. Shoulders are almost as expressive as our eyes and an important part of the upper body that you must learn to "listen" to.

Let's then move onto cues sent by the upper torso and shoulders next, but make sure to keep practicing and picking up on the cues you learned for the lower body. This chapter deals with a great deal of body language that goes from identifying your body type to understanding people's choice of clothing to sweating and causes for an upset tummy. That's right: They can all be cues to non-verbal communication.

A great example of how upper body language can influence your dealings with people is what happened to my friend Marty.

Marty had snagged an interview with a very prestigious firm and was looking forward to impressing the CEO with whom he had a meeting. Two nights before the interview, Marty received a call from his long-distance girlfriend to say she had moved on. It was a bad blow, because Marty had put in a lot of work to make the relationship last. Still, he had his interview and the chance of a fresh new beginning, or so he told himself.

At the interview, Marty answered all of the questions well, and even though the thought of his lost love lingered in his mind, he kept pushing it away and concentrating on the meeting. However, that lost love aura hung around Marty and it showed in the defeated droop of his shoulders, which the CEO noticed. Suffice to say Marty came across as unenthusiastic and was therefore not chosen. If only Marty knew that his dejected stance overshadowed the smart answers he was giving, he would have squared his shoulders and made the effort to project a confident image.

This chapter will help you to overcome situations like the one Marty faced. Learn about dressing to impress, softening the toughest of bosses to loosen up, to gain and project confidence simply through stance, and so much more.

The Hidden Language of the Upper Torso

We take upper body language for granted and don't always read much into it. Think about it, how many times have you been engaged in a conversation with someone who keeps their hand to their chest, crosses their arms to cover their chest, or gives you a pat on the back? They are a part of everyday body language that, when deciphered correctly, gives away more than you think.

Start By Identifying Your Body Type

There are three body types, also called somatotypes, and we

all belong to one, broadly understood. You will find that you fit into one of the types because you identify more with the definitions listed under that body type.

- **The Endomorph:** People with this body type complain that merely looking at food makes them gain weight. The endomorph has more than a generous portion of body fat and tends to be more muscular but is not always overweight, merely rounded. Some examples include Oprah Winfrey, Marilyn Monroe, and Beyonce–well-rounded individuals who are attractive and comfortable with their body types.
- **The Ectomorph:** These people complain about gaining weight, much to the chagrin of endomorphs. They are lean and tall, with not much muscle formation. Don't be quick to wish you were an ectomorph, as it's not always the best. Most ectomorph men wish they had broader chests and a more muscular frame, while the women long for softer curves.
- **The Mesomorphs:** These people are like the porridge that Goldilocks ate—just right. They are neither too round nor too lean. This type of frame is appropriately built and muscular. Such people can eat what they like, exercise, and easily work it off.

Since there is no hard and fast rule to say you belong exclusively to one of these body types, there are people who are a combination of two somatotypes.

- **The Endo-Endomorph:** Their lower bodies are lean, while their upper torso and midriff stores more fat. The triangular body shape is a good example of this combined body type.

- **The Ecto-Endomorph:** Pear-shaped people are good examples of this body type. They sport a lean upper body torso and a fuller rounder lower body, with plump hips and fuller thighs.

Which Body Type Do You Belong To, And Why Is It Important to Know?

Studies confirm that body types are linked to certain personality traits. Also, we unconsciously associate personality to stereotypical body shapes; hence the importance of knowing *your* body shape and being able to identify others body shapes as an important factor for reading non-verbal cues.

The following chart will throw some light on personality traits associated with each body type. This theory was put forward by W. H. Sheldon, an American psychologist who classified personality traits based on body type.

The rounder endomorphs were classed as cheerful, relaxed extroverts with tendencies to be lazy. Ectomorphs are categorized as extroverts, quiet and intelligent, while mesomorphs are labeled as being competitive, active extroverts. Now we know this theory, although true, is not 100% foolproof, because personality traits are not as cut and dry as predicted and can be intertwined as some body types are. Therefore, I invite you to take the following quiz to gain a broader understanding of your personality trait in connection to your body type.

Personality Traits Associated With Body Type

Endomorph	Mesomorph	Ectomorph
Relaxed	Energetic	Awkward
Leisurely	Dominant	Shy
Soft-hearted	Reckless	Serious
Sociable	Adventurous	Suspicious
Generous	Courageous	Anxious
Forgiving	Assertive	Tense
Contented	Optimistic	Cool
Bubbly	Competitive	Reflective
Kind	Efficient	Withdrawn
Soft-natured	Hot-tempered	Gentle-tempered

Quiz to Determine Body Shape and Personality Link (circle as many appropriate answers from those in the brackets)

1. In general, I feel (anxious, relaxed, happy, self-satisfied, energetic, shy, relaxed, and confident).
2. When I engage in work or study, I mostly feel (lazy, efficient, calm, accurate, competitive, enthusiastic, and helpful).
3. When I interact with others, I am (awkward, outgoing, gentle-natured, anxious, kind, bubbly, shy, talkative, and hot-tempered).
4. I can be described as (active, generous, forgiving, generous, bossy, outgoing, and suspicious).
5. My friends and family think I am (dominating, withdrawn, confident, outgoing, friendly, shy, and hot-tempered).

Write down your circled answers and try to gauge how closely your personality traits are associated with your body type to understand the importance of gauging body type as part of the context for reading body type.

Reading Upper Body Language

Upper body language can be negative or positive–a shrug of the shoulders, a tight bear hug or pat on the shoulder, a turn of the body, and even the clothes the person is wearing.

A person's sense of style says a lot about their personality, as well as about the context of the situation.

The Language of Clothes

Some people are required to wear a uniform to work or are expected to dress in a specific style, but when we do have a choice, the clothes we pick are a reflection of what we are feeling, or rather the emotional state we are in when we choose our outfit.

If you feel attractive and sexy, you would dress to show off your body; if you want to make a good impression and be taken seriously, you would dress in a power outfit—a suit. For times you are tired and disgruntled, you may decide that sweatpants are about the most effort you can make when it comes to getting dressed.

Conversely, women who are in the peak of their fertility period (near to ovulation) will choose to dress more provocatively as a way of courtship—think about the type of clothing people you meet at clubs and bars are wearing, and you will understand this theory better. Those people are out there to attract a potential partner because their bodies are in the fertility phase and they naturally seek companionship–a theory that studies have confirmed (Durante et al., 2008).

Established dressing styles will reflect a person's personality, and you too will have a preferred style of dress–whether the conservative dresser, the outlandish cheerful dresser, or the modern trendy dresser who likes to keep up with times.

There is a psychological theory behind the color and type of fabric you choose for your clothes, and you can use that knowledge to judge the personality of other people.

- Color: People who tend to wear darker-colored clothes are generally on the serious, professional side, while people who choose pastel shades are more friendly, warm, and easy to approach. Those who choose bold bright colors on a regular basis are confident and self-assured.
- Fabric texture: Lightweight, more breezy-looking fabrics give off a relaxed, laidback aura, while heavy thick fabrics will make you look more grave and important.

Sometimes, an individual's style will speak openly about the type of person they are.

- People who are proud of their bodies and the hard work they put into maintaining a healthy physique will wear body-hugging clothing that reveals their muscular shapes or toned bodies.
- Flamboyant people who enjoy being different will dress likewise. They choose outlandish clothing in a variety of styles and colors to create a single outfit.
- People who wish to be taken seriously, or crave authority will dress in sharp business suits, or uniforms, and will not feel shy about flaunting their achievements, such as medals, badges, etc.
- Rebellious people, such as teenagers, will choose to dress differently, sporting goth styles or overly cool casual trends. A good example of rebellious fashion used to create a shock effect is *saggers*; yes, it's a real word used to describe individuals who wear sagging

or low-rider pants that hang so low their underwear is revealed.

- The stylish dresser who wishes to impress and attract attention will use their clothes for this very purpose, just like a woman uses her swaying hips to garner attention to themselves. A sharp dresser can be a man who wants to be noticed, while a woman who chooses feminine clothing, chic dresses, and stiletto heels is trying her best to look attractive and desirable.

Bottom line: You can use clothing to impress. Tailored power suits, a smart hair style, and designer accessories will certainly create an impression. However, studies show that dressing to resemble the style of the other person has the most positive effect as it creates a sense of belonging (Fasoli et al., 2018). Therefore, no matter how unique your style is, if you seek favorable results, you may want to project a positive body language by dressing for the occasion—like everyone else.

Positive Torso Language

Positive body language puts the person in a position of power. They project likeability, look relaxed, and garner respect from others. Open body language is another name for these positive non-verbal cues, which have the power to put others around you at ease and present you as approachable. This is an essential tip for introverts, who often give off an unapproachable and awkward vibe that makes them look aloof and disinterested. However, it's a wrong perception, as most introverts are simply shy rather than aloof.

Mastering positive body language will help you to overcome these inhibitions. And the best method of learning is observing positive body language signals in other people.

Here are the most common positive upper torso body language poses.

The Bear Hug or Man Hug

A man hug is both intimate and non-sexual at the same time. It's masculine and says, *I like you a lot but let's not get too mushy about it.* A quick, rough hug, followed by a couple of pats on the back, tell you the other person is glad to see you in a totally platonic way.

Tips:

- If the other person does not initiate a hug, and you are feeling awkward to do so, a good and safe cue to show brotherly love is the fist bump. You can initiate this to break the ice and wait for the cue the other person is leaning in for a hug at the end of the fist bump.
- Sometimes, a man hug can become a close cuddle, especially if it's between two friends meeting after a long time. This does not mean there are romantic feelings involved, but simply affection that is given in a two to three-second long hug to say, *hey, I missed you bro.* It's all well within the parameters of tough masculinity, of course.

The Pat on the Back

Are you an awkward hugger? Do you wonder about when it's appropriate to let go, or if you are hugging too tight? This may not be a problem if it's your love interest. But what if it's a friend, relative, colleague, etc?

Tips:

- A good way to get a hug just right is to mirror the type of hug you get. Whether it's a tight hug, a quick

embrace, or a lingering cuddle, let the other person
take the lead.

- As for when to let go, a good signal is a pat on the
back. This is a non-verbal cue the other person
sends to say they are ready to let go. Therefore,
mirror their actions, and let go at the first series of
pats—don't end up hugging until you are given
several pats on the back that say, *hey, let go!*

The Sincere Chest Touch

Someone placing both hands on their chest while trying to
get a point across is most likely trying to reaffirm their honesty.
An effective way to practice reading this cue is to watch
someone trying to prove a point when they are being cross-
questioned. Placing both hands on the chest is indicative of
distress, and a need to prove their honesty in a situation where
they are not trusted. It's important to understand the circumstances before you make a judgment on this non-verbal signal.

Tips:

- Show empathy, not judgment
- Ask more questions to help the other person clarify
their point.

The Belly Does Not Lie

Similar to feet pointing toward someone the person is
attracted to, or find fascinating or comforting, so does the belly
button. I'm not talking about lifting up your shirt, or that of the
other person to expose belly buttons. The cue here is the stomach. If it's facing you directly, chances are the person is feeling
comfortable in your presence, is interested in what you are
saying, or is even attracted to you.

Tips:

- Use this cue to build on your self-confidence, ease into the conversation, and eliminate those awkward feelings, because the other person is telling you they like you and are interested in what you are saying.
- Let's not forget that feet are the most sensitive to inner emotions; hence, if the other person's feet are pointing away from you, although their stomach/belly button is facing you, chances are they are only mildly interested and are contemplating heading somewhere else.

THE CHEST-OUT, Standing-Tall Pose of Confidence

A person who sticks their chest out, squares their shoulders, and stands tall is probably exuding loads of self-confidence. Such people's enthusiasm is always contagious, so we often find ourselves drawn to them.

To observe this pose more, you can check out some videos of Olympic winners, as they will stand tall and proud. Conversely, you will notice that those who are defeated will slouch and try to make themselves as small as possible.

Characteristics of a pride pose:

- Chest out
- Head held high
- Broad smile that reaches the eyes
- Standing tall with broad shoulders
- Flaunting oneself and taking up space

Examples of celebrities who exude confidence are Zendaya, Kamala Harris, Tom Cruise, Jennifer Lawrence, Russel Crowe, Priyanka Chopra, and let's not forget legends like John Wayne.

Tips:

- Assume a pride pose the next time you must attend
  a function and walk into a room full of strangers or
  need to make a presentation, address an audience,
  etc. The pride pose is almost like a continuation of
  the power pose we discussed earlier. So what you do
  is practice the power pose/Wonder
  Woman/Superman pose before you go out there,
  and when you do, use a pride pose to carry you
  forward and sustain your confidence.
- Never cringe away from someone displaying a pride
  pose. If they have a puffed-out chest and are
  expanding their torso to take up more space, do not
  try to shrink in return. Reflect the pose. I'm not
  asking you to puff your chest out at them and invade
  their space, as it will only make you look aggressive;
  instead, square your shoulders, hold your head high,
  and look them in the eye to avoid feeling
  intimidated.

NEGATIVE UPPER BODY *Language*

Deciphering negative body language is important to determine your impact and success in an ongoing conversation. It's a good cue to let you know that you need to change the subject of your approach.

Touching the Chest with One Hand

If someone is talking to you while placing one hand on their chest, they are most likely feeling vulnerable and are using the action as a type of self-soothing mechanism.

Tips:

- You can make a judgment call by evaluating the
  context of the situation and what's being discussed.

The person pressing on their chest is trying to self-soothe or calm a rapidly beating heart.

- Someone who is pressing down on their chest using a few or all of their fingertips is showing signs of agitation as they are deeply distressed. This is your cue to evaluate the situation to try and understand the cause and help where possible.

Crossing the Arms Across the Chest

This is a defense mechanism, with the arms acting as a kind of armor that guards against threats.

When Malcolm found a dent on the back buffer of his car, he stormed into the house to confront his wife, Jessica.

"Where and when did you manage to damage my car?" he demanded.

Jessica, who was preparing breakfast, turned around, crossed her arms against her chest, and demanded.

"What makes you so sure that *I* damaged the car?" And so began a very long argument.

But here, you can see Jessica quickly jump into a defensive mode by crossing her arms against her chest. She has closed herself from attack and is initiating a protective cover, using the upper torso, which is often the first part of our body we cover.

Tips:

- Pay careful attention to this body language, it tells you when you are not getting through to someone because they disagree and have closed themselves off from what you are saying—they don't like it. It could be a customer who is presenting a proposal, telling you that they disagree with your pitch, or a disagreeing friend you are asking for a favor: "Can we change the roster so that I work Monday to Thursday, and you work Friday to Sunday?"

- The gesture can also be interpreted as a self-soothing mechanism. Because the other person is literally hugging themselves. This means you need to stop and evaluate your approach. Perhaps you are being too aggressive and demanding.

In either case, reevaluate the situation, change your tactics, and approach because, chances are, crossed arms are not going to work in your favor.

- Trick them into uncrossing their arms. Since our body has the ability to send signals to our brains (Tipper et al., 2015), you can pull down a person's non-verbal defense mechanism by getting them to uncross their arms. Let's say you have a client with arms crossed and a head nodding "no" to your proposal. Go ahead and hand them a sheet of statistics to prove your point. To read it, they must uncross their arms, which then makes them psychologically open to your proposal because they are now in the open-body pose.

Testosterone-Fueled Chest Puff

Similar to the pride pose, a puffed-out chest is a show of power, but in this case, the person is adopting a threatening stance. This non-verbal body language can take place during an aggressive situation, an argument, a pre-fight stance, etc.

The pose fuels the secretion of testosterone. The male hormone produced in the testicles represents virility and strength. Women, too, produce testosterone in small doses within the ovaries. Testosterone, among its other functionalities, stimulates the competitive streak in both sexes (van Anders et al., 2015). Puffing out the chest makes people look bigger and more powerful—winning factors in a fight.

Tips:

- Stand your ground. Do not try to shrink your body, but do not puff your chest out in return, unless, of course, you are hungry for a fight—doing so, you are challenging them. Try your best to deflate the situation by standing your ground without appearing weak or feeling inadequate.
- Use the open palms stance to show them you are not a threat. Hold up your arms and turn your open palms toward them. It says *I'm not a threat*. It's a well-accepted sign of peace that you can use at any time to deflate a hostile situation.

Goosebumps

Sudden shivering, the appearance of goosebumps, or the shakes are signals to say the person is experiencing a form of anxiety or fear.

Did you know that anxiety or fear causes hyperventilation, which means our normal blood flow is disrupted, causing a temperature drop? Thus, we actually do feel cold due to a stressful situation (Pouga et al., 2010).

Seeing these cues in someone will tell you they are distressed, and their body is automatically responding to the situation. And if you observe closely, you may catch that microexpression of fear—a fleeting show of distress that crosses the face. If, at first, you miss these subtle and fleeting shifts in facial expressions, don't worry: The more you practice putting your body language reading skills to the test, the sharper you become.

The Jacket Buttoning Cue

It's another defense mechanism quite similar to folded arms. Buttoning a jacket is creating a barricade of protection. People feeling insecure at a function may do so, while those who want to create an aura of formality may choose to button their jackets to look more professional. It could also mean they are trying to appear important to impress.

Buttoning a jacket can even be a show of respect, kind of like a man putting on a shirt to cover his upper body in the presence of a lady. Buttoning a jacket is a formal way of showing respect, perhaps to a boss or client at a meeting.

Tips:

- If you are unsure about how formal an event you have to attend is going to be, go there with a buttoned-up jacket to give a non-verbal signal of respect. If you decide it's not as ceremonious as you thought, all you have to do is unbutton your jacket.
- You can even use the buttoned-up jacket as a way to make a person feel at ease. Let's say you are on a date; casually unbuttoning your jacket tells the other person you are getting comfy in their company and settling down. The action helps ease any tension that may prevail.

Stretching

Stretching is a signal to say the person is trying to overcome tension caused by stress because stretching helps dispel the pressure that builds up in the neck and shoulder areas. Emotional stress can trigger a hormonal response from your nervous system, which, in turn, leads to a decreased blood flow caused by constricted blood vessels that result in aching muscles. Involuntary stretching is an automatic reaction to the pressure you feel in these muscles because doing so helps restore proper blood flow, thus reducing the stiffness and pain caused by stress (Teixeira et al., 2017).

Tips:

- Not only is stretching a cue for you to understand the other person is dealing with emotional anxieties, but it's also a method to help you relieve your own emotional stress.
- Stretch first thing in the morning to get your blood flowing and to soothe your aches and pains. The ten-minute *Surya Namaskar* (check out the easy-to-follow videos online) routine is a popular stretching exercise that you can practice first thing in the morning to give yourself a boost at the start of the day.

Gearing Up for Fight or Flight—Heavy Breathing

A classic signal that someone's buttons are being pushed to the limit is when their nostrils flare and their breathing becomes labored. It's an automatic reaction to the flight or fight mode our bodies go into when distressed.

Seeing this cue is a heads-up to try and cool the situation if you are in an argument with the other person. Another sign that someone is at the boiling point is their chest rising and falling rapidly.

Similarly, if you witness someone beating their chest–no, not like Tarzan, but tapping their chest lightly with their fist–it's a classic signal they are gearing up for a fight.

Tips:

- Avoid a fight by avoiding eye contact. Try to appear as small as possible, and do not engage the other person by displaying any type of power pose.
- Turn your body away from them, after which you can walk away, avoiding any regrettable confrontations.

The Subtle Power Play—Hand Placed on the Back

A guiding hand at your back may look like a gentle guide, as when walking someone out or into a meeting, for example. However, the gesture is more than a simple guide, but rather a bid for dominance and power. The person using their hand on the other person's back as though to guide them is asserting their power as the stronger of the two. This pose is also used by politicians who wish to establish their dominance over a weaker opponent.

Tips:

- Use the move to subtly establish your power. But make sure to use the move in the correct context. For example, do not use this high-power gesture with an equally dominant personality, or else you will end up in a power play.
- One of the best times to use this non-verbal cue is when you are walking someone out. Do so by gently placing your hand at the small of their back—mind you, it's a gentle touch; you are not shoving the other person out.

The Upset Stomach

Stress, panic, fear, etc., trigger a fight or flight reaction, and one way your body deals with this threat is to divert blood flow to your muscles in preparation for the great escape. When doing so, blood flow in your stomach is reduced, which means the digestive process is disrupted. Your stomach feels tight—aka butterflies! This simple reaction is what causes flutters in your stomach.

Sometimes it may lead to an upset tummy, or even vomiting. Each person's stomach will react differently when it's upset. In some cases, embarrassing acts, such as passing urine due to sudden fear or anxiety, or even relieving bowels (oops), will take place because your stomach's digestive process was disrupted, which is very upsetting. A good example is someone suddenly developing the runs before a race–it's a nervous reaction that automatically empties the bowels.

Tips:

- Okay, so you can't read this cue literally. Unless someone vomits in front of you out of sheer distress, you don't see the butterflies in their stomach or the fact they are dealing with diarrhea as a nervous reaction.
- What you can look for are signs of discomfort, such as someone running to the toilet following a stressful event or crossing their legs as though they desperately need to get to a restroom.

Nervous Sweating

Just because someone sweats, you can't jump to the conclusion they are nervous. Because genetics determine how much a person sweats and from where.

However, studies prove that fear or nervous sweat has a certain odor to it, and we can smell that fear in the sweat of the other person, thus stimulating the amygdala and hypothalamus to respond to a fearful or threatening situation (de Groot et al., 2020). So, yes, it's true we *can* smell fear.

Tips:

- Don't automatically assume someone is sweating because they are nervous or lying. Some people simply sweat more profoundly than others. So, how to tell if it's nervous sweat? You certainly cannot go sniffing at someone who is sweating to determine if they smell of fear.
- Use the context of the situation to make a judgment, which will be easier if the person is known. For

example, if you suddenly see nervous sweating in someone you generally regard as *cool-as-a-cucumber*, chances are they are undergoing sudden distress, fear, guilt, etc. It's tougher to gauge in individuals you just met; therefore, look for other signs of nervousness, coupled with sweating, to make a judgment.

Disrespectful Splaying

Do you know people who sit with their legs and arms spread out? They are not adopting a power pose; they are simply showing you their rebellious nature. Anyone with teenagers will agree and understand how splaying works.

Adult people who decide to spread themselves out are on a mission to fight against authority or to project a don't care attitude. Often, they are adults who have not overcome their adolescent habits.

Tips:

- When you notice someone splaying, try to diminish the space they have to spread themselves out; perhaps stand or sit close to them. It's a subtle sign to take back authority. This method works well for parents of rebellious teens.
- Use a power pose, or even a pride pose, to let them know they are not intimidating you, by overpowering their actions through counteractions.

Expressive Shoulders

Let's move to the shoulders next, one of the more expressive parts of the upper torso. Our shoulders are very flexible therefore, we have learned to use them to project several cues.

- Annoyance
- Dejection
- Flirtation
- A signal to confirm consent
- Confusion

These are some of the messages we project through our shoulders.

The Professional and Strong Shoulder Stance

"Sit up straight, don't slouch," you may have been told several times by adults when growing up. This is because good posture is measured through your shoulders. Squared shoulders, with a straight neck, give off an aura of authority and power.

You look professional, strong, and capable. Have you ever seen a military type with slumped shoulders? I think not. That's because no one in the military is allowed to have droopy shoulders—they need to project power and professionalism, and shoulders back is the best stance to do so.

- Someone who suddenly squares their shoulders and sits up straight is saying *okay, I have decided*. Such gestures are seen in response to someone suddenly making a decision.
- Squared shoulders signal determination to stick to their guns.
- Moments people feel proud of themselves, their children, and so on, they stand to be noticed with squared shoulders.
- A person trying to impress someone: Think of the young man who suddenly stands up straight, shoulders back to look impressive to the attractive girl walking past him.

Observe and use the context of the situation to make a judgment.

The Flirtatious Shoulder

That's right, a shoulder can be used to flirt. This one is perfected by females who use shoulder movements to appear coy.

- Raised shoulders and a slight turn of the head in your direction are indicative of attraction, as well as an invitation to say, *come on over.*
- Slightly elevated shoulders, followed by a flirty side glance, mean you are on their radar, and it's safe to assume she is being mischievously flirty with you. Check the eyebrows–if they are raised, and she is biting on her lip, then bam, you are one lucky guy!

Fake Vs Real Mirth Through Raised Shoulders

I often wonder if people understand some of the jokes I make because although they laugh, I am left with a nagging feeling they are being pretentious. Then I discovered this marvelous cue for reading body language to know if I was really that funny.

- Watch out for the raised shoulders whenever someone laughs, and you know they are genuinely delighted. People who fake laughter do not extend the gesture to their shoulders.

The Super Fast Shoulder Shrug

"Jonathan, do you know why John is missing from work today?" asked his manager.

John and Jonathan were best pals, but the latter's lightning-quick shoulder shrug told their manager that Jonathan genuinely did not know.

- This is what that quick shoulder shrug means—they really don't know.
- It's a positive non-verbal cue that's indicative of honesty.

The Shrug

While a quick shoulder shrug screams honesty, others may not be so straightforward.

- Confusion is depicted in someone who raises both shoulders together, keeps them raised for around two to three seconds, then brings them down.

"Carol, do you think taking route 31 will get us faster to the party?" Up went Carol's shoulders in slow motion to say, she was not sure about the route.

Add raised palms to this gesture, and the person is telling you they have nothing to hide.

If the eyebrows are raised as the shoulder shrugs, they are showing compliance.

"Okay, I am taking route 31; the map says it's faster. Is that okay?" Carol shrugged her shoulders in compliance and said, "No worries, go right ahead; you're the navigator."

- Indifference is displayed if someone raises one shoulder, while the other remains relaxed, as a way of telling you that they really don't care or can't be bothered.

"Would you like pizza or hot dogs for dinner?" Mom asked her teen daughter, who gave her the classic *whatever* half-shoulder shrug.

The Aggressive Shoulder Roll

Think about those fight scenes you see in movies, where the

tough guys circle around the puny guy, rolling his neck and shoulders, as if to say, *I'm ready to pulverize you.*

Or how about the time you see someone at the end of a long day roll their shoulders and sigh in relief? Clearly, they are done for the day and need to relax.

A shoulder role can be an aggressive signal, or it can mean that the person needs to de-stress.

Soothing the Shoulder

People sometimes talk while massaging their shoulders. They will knead the shoulder on the right side with the left hand, and vice-versa. Such people are using a straightforward signal to say they need to de-stress or are fatigued.

This is also a self-soothing gesture to relieve sudden anxiety brought on by a conversation or act.

The area that gets massaged is generally between the collarbone (clavicle) and the muscle we use to shrug the shoulder (*levator scapulae*). It's a highly receptive area that's sensitive to pain since the muscle tightens when stressed. Likewise, the area is receptive to touch. Therefore, people are able to soothe themselves by massaging the region.

- Since a sudden feeling of anxiety brought on by a discussion or situation will instigate this self-soothing action, you must watch for the cue, the part of the conversation, or action, that triggers the shoulder rub.
- People who are under extreme pressure and need to relax will attempt to do so by giving themselves a massage–rubbing the most sensitive and also the most tensed-up part of their body–mid-conversation. It's a non-verbal action that says, *okay, let's wrap things up; I'm tired.*

The Stoop

Children are very graphic and will stomp around, stoop their shoulders, looking mournful when they don't get what they want. As adults, we cannot be so "childish" (well, not always), so we resort to subtle non-verbal gestures that say we are depressed, feeling anxious, or are trying to hide something —and shoulders play a starring role.

- Depression over time leads to a person developing a stoop. The more hopeless they feel, the more they hunch their shoulders until they develop a permanent stoop of the bent neck and rounded shoulders when walking.
- The phone hunch. Not only are we bent at the neck when flipping through our smartphones, but we also hunch our shoulders. The latter is indicative of guarding privacy. A good method to avoid a hunch caused by your phone is to hold it at eye level. However, you may then feel as though your activity on your phone is exposed to anyone peering over your shoulder. My solution to avoiding a permanent hunch is to limit phone time in public when you are most likely to hunch over the device.
- The secretive hunch. A hunch naturally covers a person's chest area, and we already established that covering the chest region is an act of self-defense. Therefore, a person hunching is being secretive or is on the defensive.

As always, you need to evaluate and understand the *circumstance* leading to the action before making a judgment.

The Language of the Neck

Necks are very expressive; they can be long and lean or short and almost invincible. Necks are very sexual, highly sensual, and attractive. This is because the neck is home to a lot of nerve endings that make the area extremely sensitive to touch—this is why neck kissing is a huge part of foreplay.

The Karen Tribe in Thailand are a good example, as they value elongated necks. Long necks are considered elegant and beautiful among them, which leads to women adding rings to their necks in a bid to elongate their necks further to an almost unnatural length. But I do wonder about the result of covering up all those sensitive nerve endings with metal rings.

While the Karen tribe uses metal rings to highlight their necks, the rest of us use subtle gestures, such as covering up or exposing our necks—depending on the situation. Have you noticed how people place a hand to their neck and cover it when nervous, while conversely, an attractive woman will boldly display her neck as part of a courtship ritual?

Just like the hundreds of nerve endings present in the neck, neck body language too can be complex. Let's explore.

Showing Off the Neck

When Holly met Sean on a blind date, she was wearing a scarf around her neck and was rather apprehensive about dinner with a total stranger. But as the evening wore on, and Sean had her giggling with his friendly and hilarious banter, Holly began to feel relaxed and found herself attracted to the gentle, interesting man sitting in front of her. Unconsciously, she unwound the scarf and hung it on the back of her chair, and as she fell deeper into conversation with Sean, Holly kept tilting her head, exposing the side of her neck, and even ran one hand along the length of one side. This was an automatic reaction, where Holly was using her pretty neck to flirt with

Sean, who, of course, took the bait and found himself wanting to ask Holly out on a second date.

Flirtation is not all that neck exposure is good for.

- Exposing the neck with a side tilt of the head, and winning a smile, will help diffuse a volatile situation. Use the trick to say *I'm a lover, not a fighter*, the next time you face an aggressive situation.
- The neck is seen as a soothing part of the body; babies tend to snuggle into the neck of adults to feel safe and fall asleep. Even older children lay their heads against a parent's neck to rest when tired and traveling. Therefore, neck exposure has the power to pacify.

Neck Touching

Quite similar to showing off the neck in a flirtatious gesture, touching the neck can indicate attraction.

If a woman wants to appear sultry, she will feel her neck, around the area of her Adam's apple, in a bid to look sexy. You can use the same gesture if you want to appear more attractive, but mind you use it at the right place and at the right time—for example, stroking your neck while presenting the annual budget will not make people ignore the huge deficit in the entertainment budget.

Otherwise, a woman may feel her neck in the company of a date she feels nervous about. The gesture says she's anxious for the meet-up to go well.

People stroking their necks can indicate stress, too, since the gesture is a self-soothing mechanism. Therefore, judging these moves in context is very important.

The Sensitive Jugular Notch or Neck Dimple

Your jugular notch is that small, indented space you find at the base of the neck right between the collar bones. It's more pronounced in some people and hardly visible in others. But it's there, and we are aware of it, especially females. Some people call it the neck dimple, which is a more romantic-sounding name.

Did you know that massaging your neck dimple (or suprasternal notch if you want to get scientific) has the psychological power to soothe? This is one reason that makes some people rub the area whenever they are feeling anxious or panicked; the action is more common among women who self-soothe by rubbing this inverted area at the base of their neck.

Touching the jugular notch indicates

- nervousness
- fear
- uncertainty
- On some occasions, a lie—a person who repeatedly touches their neck dimple when answering a question is quite likely lying. You can use this knowledge in context to judge a situation.

Touching the jugular notch is not wholly feminine, for men do it too, except they will not be gentle like women. Instead, they will grab the spot with their hand and perhaps pull at the skin. Although different, the action has the same non-verbal cues as when a woman touches her neck dimple.

Playing With Neck Accessories

There are people who talk while twirling their necklaces about, or they will pull their ties, smooth them down, or wave them about. Others may play with the collar of their shirts. These are all accessories located around the neck. And quite similar to rubbing the neck, they are using these accessories as a non-verbal gesture to say they feel nervous.

The new intern, on the first day of his job, will play around with his tie, or the lady waiting to meet the bank manager about a loan may nervously pull at her necklace.

Conversely, a woman may use her chain-pulling techniques to draw a man's attention to her neck—that's right, women are pretty forward when it comes to promoting their necks. After all, the neck is a highly sexual and sensual part of the body.

The Head Flip

Recall a particular scene in a movie where the femme-fatale flips back her head, hair flying sideways, to reveal her neck as she looks up at the male hero with a beguiling smile. There's no hidden message here–she's giving him the green light, instead of hiding her intentions. Go ahead and use the extended neck and head flip during a conversation, to let someone you are interested in or attracted to them. My advice is to practice in front of a mirror, so you don't appear as though you are suffering from a neck sprain.

But hold on before you go, leaning into someone flipping their head up at you! If the action follows a frown, chances are they are asserting their power over you, and the head flip that stretches the neck out is a ploy to make them look taller and more intimidating.

Stalling—The Neck Stretch

"Adam, did you finally get the promotion?" Adam's wife asked him as he walked in the door.

Adam stopped, took off his coat, and stretched his neck from side to side as though he was relieving tension. It's a common gesture we see people do. Mostly males. Adam, of course, did not get the promotion. He used the neck stretch to stall for time and formulate a suitable answer.

People stretch their necks when they

- need time to answer a stressful question.
- are anxious and confused about how to deal with a situation.

- or are simply trying to get the tension out of their necks by stretching them. Holding the neck down in a stretch is a great stress reliever (Tunwattanapong et al., 2015), and we often do this by moving our heads side-to-side, forward, and back, especially after spending time hunched over a computer or smartphone.

Stretching the Collar—The Cool Down Mechanism

People who are angry or frustrated will suddenly feel hot under the collar. At these times, they may adjust their clothing. Stretch out the collar, pull at a neckband in a kind of airing out gesture, or even unbutton the top button of a shirt, and fan themselves around the neck.

These gestures all mean the same thing–the person is angry, exasperated, overwhelmed, and trying to get their emotions under control.

The Gulp or Quick Swallow

Do you notice how, when talking to someone, they suddenly swallow hard enough to make their Adam's apple bob up and down? That's a hard swallow, a gesture that indicates the person is feeling uncomfortable or telling a lie. How do you figure out which it is? Well, it depends on the question. Someone preparing to lie will often swallow hard before answering.

Panic is another reason that people suddenly swallow in a gulping movement. Panic or anxiety can cause a person's throat to go dry, which makes them swallow hard, causing the rapid movement of the Adam's apple.

The Adam's apple is a great tool for detecting deception, so some security experts, such as airport personnel, are trained to watch out for these nervous gestures among passengers who may be carrying illegal items.

The Disagreeing Neck

People will often use non-verbal communication to let us know they don't agree with what we are saying. Just as someone uses their eyes to look over your shoulder, or crosses their arms to show resistance, so too can the neck be used to say, *sorry man, I disagree!*

Here are the cues someone disagrees with what you're saying.

- Scratching the side of the neck toward the back of the ear is indicative of a disagreement. Watch for the cue, as it can be helpful if you are dealing with a client or proposing an action plan to a friend who is perhaps too polite to let you know they don't want to spend the weekend helping you clean out your garage.
- The *oh no!* stiffening of the neck indicates sudden alertness.

"Hey Bob, I bought us tickets to the opera!" Bob stopped eating, sat up straight, squared his shoulders, and looked up at Tracy, neck straight and eyes unwavering—he did *not* want to attend the opera!

The Pain-In-the-Neck Gesture

"Howard, did you take out the garbage?" asked Mary. Howard answered with a quick slap to the back of his neck and went out of the room. What Howard literally told Mary was, *you can be a real pain, and no, I did not, and I don't want to bother with taking the garbage out.* Of course, Howard did take out the garbage because his negativity was only communicated non-verbally.

Another gesture that indicates someone is stressed is tugging at the bottom of their chin. A more male action occurs when the person will skin down as though they are trying to extend their chins. The more they pull, the higher their levels of stress.

THE NEGATIVE NECK **Rub**

Not every neck rub is a come-hither coy pose. Sometimes it can signal negativity, stress, and insecurity. People with low self-esteem will often rub the back of their necks, increasing their sense of negativity. If someone is rubbing the back of their neck, chances are they are critical by nature. So, watch out.

Stress can make a person rub the side or front of their neck. Especially rubbing your neck on the right side is a self-soothing gesture because the action stimulates what's called your vagus nerve. These nerves are a part of the human parasympathetic nervous system, so massaging this area will trigger a reduction in heart rate, offering a soothing effect (Howland, 2014).

Have you ever envisioned the neck to have such a complicated range of communication? Well, it does, and just like feet, the neck is a pretty accurate part of the body to judge non-verbal cues, so just make sure you get the context of the situation right.

4

THE LANGUAGE OF ARMS, HANDS, AND FINGERS

Authenticity doesn't just mean you're not filtering what you're saying, it's about being able to know and access the best parts of yourself and bring them forward. —Amy Cuddy

Hands on her hips, Megan stood her ground and glared silently at the man who had just jumped the line in front of her at the bank.

"What do you think you are doing?" she asked softly, not wanting to create a scene. The man just looked away and pretended to not hear her. She held out her arms, palms out, and then dropped them to her sides in a helpless, defeated gesture and said, "I've been in this line for twenty minutes and I need to get back to work. Please take your correct place at the back of the line."

However, the rude stranger simply gave her a haughty look and ignored her plea. He knew from her body language that she wasn't the type to make a scene.

The bank manager, seated too far to hear what was being said, was watching Megan, who stood there, her hands on her hips, followed by a dejected stance as her shoulders stooped, and her hands splayed out to display defeat and disbelief.

Walking up to Meghan, he discreetly asked her if there was a problem. She reluctantly pointed at the man in front of her and said, "It's no big deal, but he jumped the line, and my lunch break is almost done."

"Please follow me miss," said the manager as he escorted Meghan to an empty teller window, called over one of the tellers, and asked them to assist the young miss who was in a hurry.

Now, Meghan had made no scene or raised her voice; it was her body language, specifically, her arm gestures, that told the manager something was not right.

Our arms, hands, and fingers can be quite expressive. They can threaten, plead, applaud or be sensual. In this chapter, we will learn about interpreting all those signals you are faced with on a daily basis.

Arms That Talk

I know most people pay attention to the eyes and facial expressions as the best way to catch those microscopic reactions, and to look for non-verbal cues. But I have always found arms to be pretty explicit about what's going on with a person, especially if the person is someone who uses their arms very expressively— you know, the kind that are very graphic waving their arms about as they speak.

Happiness and excitement, even anger which creates a rush of adrenaline, make us spread our arms out, expanding ourselves to make us look bigger and noticeable.

"Hey, man you want to mess with *me*?" asked the huge bodybuilder, spreading out his arms to show off his muscular torso.

Conversely, when we feel anxious or nervous, we will try to look smaller, and to do so, we try to hide our arms–placing them behind our backs, folding them across our chests in a defensive mode, or pasting them to our sides when seated or standing.

"Er, no mister, I'm sorry," said Howard, looking up at the huge angry bodybuilder, as he folded his arms back, took a step back, and looked around for an escape route.

Apart from how expansive arms are to judge a person's thoughts and emotions, we can decipher arm language by how smooth they are. A confident person will have a smooth flow to their arms, such as a professional cook doing a cookery demonstration making his favorite cake. But take, for instance, someone trying to throw a cloth over a spider they are scared of, and they would have jittery arm movements showcasing the person's nervousness and fear.

Arms That Are in Charge or Spell Defiance

A person of authority will stand with their hands on their hips and elbows out. The pose makes them look bigger, and when coupled with a stern look, intimidating. The pose used to express power is a projection of dominance by a very confident person.

This pose is known as arms akimbo and can also indicate defiance, so must be used carefully in case you don't want to project the wrong image. Sometimes we tend to stand arms akimbo because it's a comfortable pose, but at the wrong time and in the wrong situation, you could be sending a message of defiance or power.

For example, the teenager who refuses to apologize because they did nothing wrong will place their hands akimbo and argue their case. This pose will not only make them look defiant, but also irritates parents, who see it as a defiance of their authority.

Arms Are Used to Express Thoughts, Emotions, and Moods

Paying careful attention to how much arms expand is important for judging a person's thoughts, feelings, and emotions.

Expansive Arms

Show a kid a room decorated for their birthday, and they will clap their hands with joy. Or watch people cheer as their favorite football team wins the Superbowl, and chances are they will be waving their arms above their heads in joy.

Arms that open out wide to draw the other person into their personal space show love, such as when we are greeting an old friend or family member. You can tell if it's a *hello* or *goodbye* hug by the duration. The hello hug is held for longer, while the goodbye hug is quick since they have already been preparing for the departure.

Someone who is angry will hold up one arm, palms out, to indicate, *enough, stop talking*! Or they would extend their arm toward the exit in a *please leave* gesture.

Sometimes, both arms held up indicate defeat; okay, *you got me, I give up*! To determine the meaning behind the raised arms, you need to look for facial expressions, a defeated look in this case.

Constricted Arms

A nervous and insecure person will stand with their arms down and in front of their body as they lock hands right in front of their genital area. Remember the fig leaf stance we mentioned earlier? This signifies they are protecting their most vulnerable areas since they feel tense and exposed (not literally).

Crossed Arms

Angry people may fold their arms across their chest in defiance to indicate they do not agree and have closed off their minds to the conversation. This type of crossed-arm gesture is done with the hands tucked out and gripping the top of the arm. Or they will use the same gesture when sad but will couple the folded arms, with a bent head and slouched shoulders, to make them look smaller.

Crossed arms can also signify comfort, as someone who is feeling cold will tuck their hands inside their crossed arms. The same gesture can signify contentment as well. Someone who is sitting will try to get comfy by crossing their arms and leaning back.

Crossed arms help increase concentration. Do you tend to do this when trying to solve a problem or when paying attention to a certain task, such as standing at a meeting? Crossed arms have been shown to create changes in the brain that influence cognitive behavior and decision-making (Ora et al., 2016).

Watch out for secretive crossed arms. Check for how expansive the person's arms are when they cross them. If the elbows and upper arms are further out, they are happy to see you. But the closer the upper arms are to their body, the more secretive the person is or less happy the person is to see you.

The Flirtatious Arm Gesture

People attracted to each other will often sit close, and their arms will be touching. One classic gesture is placing their arms around each other's shoulders. This is probably because touch causes the bonding hormone oxytocin to be released. It's what bonds mothers to their babies, and couples can feel this same rush of togetherness through touch. Touching arms is a nonsexual gesture that can be practiced in public, and couples enjoy the feeling of love the release of oxytocin elicits; plus, as a result of oxytocin being released, other feel-good hormones, such as serotonin and dopamine, the reward hormone, are secreted.

Arms That Signal Power, Ownership, and Aggression

Arms can be territorial, as when the boyfriend slips his arm around his girlfriend's shoulder to let others know she is with him. Also, think of the boss who sits with his arms spread across the back of the sofa to say, well, he's the boss, and he is in charge. Or he may sit slightly away from the table, leaning back with his arms spread out and resting on the chair's armrest. In all of these cases, arms help to display confidence.

People of authority will avoid folding their arms across their chests because they are in control and have nothing to hide. Such people will greet others and stand with their arms by their side, or even place their hands in their pockets, expanding their torso as their elbows jut out, which also signals detachment. Taking this signal of detachment further, the "boss" may choose to take a step back from a group of employees to signal he is on a different level.

Arms can guard territory or privacy. For example, think of times you've seen the military intervene by locking arms to form a barricade when trying to push back a crowd. Likewise, someone who doesn't want to be approached or consoled will hold out their arms to say *stay back*. The same message can be sent through arms crossed against the chest, thus forming a barrier, and indicating the person's reluctance to engage with anyone.

People who perceive themselves as important and powerful will try to make themselves look bigger by spreading out their arms and legs in an opposite manner to when they express happiness. This type of arm-spreading is aggressive and demanding, and through practice, you will be able to pick up the differences.

Bracing one's arms can also be interpreted as an aggressive or defensive act. Much like a pair of boxers getting ready for their fight by raising their arms, a person doing so can be perceived as getting ready to defend themselves or preparing to attack.

Arms That Show Defeat, No-Confidence, and Nervousness

People who feel negatively about themselves will try to look smaller, so they go unnoticed. One method is to tuck their arms behind their back and stand with their shoulders drooped. They are trying to shrink themselves and go unnoticed.

Similarly, someone waiting to be called in for an interview will be seated with their arms pressed tightly to their sides, or on their lap hands, tightly gripping each hand for reassurance. The gestures signal nervousness and insecurity.

The Self-Hug

How about the times you sat at the dentist's reception waiting your turn to get that root canal work done? Did you indulge in a self-assuring hug?

This gesture involves crossing your arms and using the left hand to grip the top of the right arm, and vice versa. Two things happen here. First, the person indulging in this gesture is protecting their upper body by creating a barricade with their arms, and second, they are giving themselves a hug. Depending on how bad the situation is (like a pending root canal), the hug will be tighter, sometimes to the extent of the knuckles becoming white because of the tight grip.

The half hug is more common among females. It's a more subtle form of self-soothing, reminiscent of when they were held as a baby. The half hug happens with one arm folded across the torso, and the elbow of the other resting on that arm, while the hand, or fist, offers support to the chin or face. It signifies a lack of confidence but is also used as a comforting and comfortable pose.

Another variation of the one-arm self-hug is to fold one arm across the belly and grip the upper arm of the other, which is hanging down.

Touching Arms to Establish a Link

Just as lovers use touch to bond, you can use touch to form

a connection with someone in a totally non-romantic way. But where and when you touch is of the utmost importance—especially if you want to avoid being chased by a mob and labeled a weirdo.

A light touch helps establish rapport with the other person, and the safest place to do so is the elbow, upper arm, and shoulder. And no, you don't feel them up; instead, practice a light tap, or slight touch with your fingertips; the touch should not linger for more than a second. This type of body language signals trust and matters when forming new alliances.

Exposing Arms

A well-built man will garner a lot of attention by exposing his muscular arms, but apart from their sexual appeal, bare arms can send other signals.

Someone who is rolling up their sleeves is either saying, *hey, look at me, and my sexy arms*, or *okay, it's time to get down to some work*. This is literally practiced in movies, where getting down to some work is dramatized through the rolling up of shirt sleeves.

Then again, rolling up the sleeves can be a subtle metaphor to indicate that what the person is about to undertake is tough, and they are not all that confident.

As always, it's important to understand the context of the situation before making a judgment call.

Let's Get Handsy

The language of hands is highly fascinating, as they are the most verbal part of our body—and the most hardworking, since hands, have the power to influence what's being said and even change the outcome of a situation. Therefore, it's important to pay careful attention to hand signals to avoid misinterpreting any cues and to learn about using them for your benefit.

Here are a few handy facts to keep in mind (I love puns)!

- Using hand gestures increases the attention paid to your speech—people listen better to someone using hand gestures. It's as if hand gestures enhance what you are saying.
- Hand gestures aid your speech. They help you to formulate your words and get the correct thoughts out of your head and into your speech.
- Hands gestures stimulate the thinking process, just like when as a kid, you used your hands to solve math problems.

How to Use Your Hand Gestures Successfully

The success of anything lies in not overdoing it, and when it comes to hand gestures, this is an important factor to keep in mind. Remember: You are having a conversation, giving a speech, presentation, etc. You are not singing in the opera—therefore, you don't need elaborate hand gestures.

By "elaborate," I mean raising your hands above your head as you speak in a very expansive manner. By doing so, you are creating drama with your hands, and people will be following those movements to see if you are going to eventually flap your arms and fly away, instead of listening to what you are saying. Remember: Your hands must enhance your words—they are the non-verbal tone enhancers to your speech.

Here's how I have classified different hand gestures after years of paying attention to body language.

- The passive tuck: The person talking prefers to fold their arms in a no-nonsense stance as they speak.
- The actor: This person is overdramatizing what they are saying with their hands. Their arms will fly up

above their heads or spread out like an eagle's wings as they try to animate what they are saying.

- The descriptive talker: This person uses their hands to merely enhance their words and will not be overly dramatic or too passive. They are using their hands to support what they are saying.

Descriptive talkers are the most effective, as their hand gestures do not out-talk their verbal dialogue. There is a simple rule to being a descriptive talker, and that is to make sure not to be too expansive or too constrictive.

Don't hug your hands to your body while speaking, nor should you raise them above your chest level or lower them below your waist. Imagine a safe zone, a kind of box that extends to your chest level and waist.

How to Use Hand Gestures Successfully

Let's face it, not all of us are handsy talkers; some of us feel downright awkward to be waving our arms and hands about as we speak. But learning to skillfully use your hands to articulate what you are saying has many benefits; plus, it's been scientifically proven that gestures help influence thought and change minds (Goldin-Meadow, 2014). Isn't that awesome?

Here are some tips to keep in mind when initiating hand gestures.

- Match your hand language to your words and not vice-versa. People who are stuck for words will overcompensate with hand gestures.

"You know what I mean, right, about how awkward Sheril can be?" Gracie said as she shifted her arms up and down and expanded her palms. Her hand gestures told the rest of the story about Sheril's awkwardness. But the person she was talking to did not know how Sheril could be awkward and was therefore already considering Gracie an *exaggerator* in their mind.

Know exactly what you want to say. If it's a speech, study it; if it's research, know your subject, etc. In doing some home-work, you avoid trying to fill the silence with hand language.

- Practice in front of a mirror until you are satisfied your hand gestures are natural and have a smooth flow. Forced or jerky hand and arm gestures will make you look like a robot.
- Ask a friend to record a speech you give or even a casual conversation you are having with someone. It's a good method to analyze your body language, understand your signature moves, and even fine-tune some of them.
- Make sure to use the correct hand gestures. Apart from cultural differences, there are some hand signals that give different meanings in different situations. Therefore, it's important that your gestures justify and match the context of the situation.

Reading Hand Gestures and Learning About the Most Influential Cues

1. Grab attention—the *listen-up folks* hand signal!

Let's say you need to stand up in front of a crowd and make a speech, or you are in a circle of friends and must make an important announcement. Use the attention-grabbing signal, which is to have an outstretched arm and palm up, which you slap with the back of the palm on your other hand. It's like an outstretched arm, palm-up clap. This is a powerful signal and should not be used lightly.

"We need to change our return policies *now*, to keep up with the competition," the store manager reiterated firmly as she called attention to her words, slapping the palm of her hand with the back of her other hand.

1. Indicating Numbers

Add clarity to what you are saying, and also grab attention, by showing the number you are talking about with your fingers.

"Let's move onto the very interesting point three," she said, holding up three fingers.

1. The Fist Shake

This hand signal signifies confidence and resolve.

Max shook his fist in the air and hollered, "This time, we must win the election by a landslide!"

Make sure to use this powerful gesture with care; if you couple it with a high tone or aggressive type of voice, you can look threatening to some people.

1. Downplay your comment

Reiterate that what you are saying is not really important, or that you are talking about a very minor incident, with this hand gesture. Take your thumb and index finger and act as though you are holding a grain of sand in between their tips.

"I've got just one last, very casual and small point to make, kids, and then you can go," the principal reassured the assembly as he held up his fingers as though he was holding a pea in between them.

1. Making a *Wise* Gesture

Well, it's universally recognized as a wise gesture when you press the tips of your fingertips on each hand together to form a steeple as you sit ramrod straight, looking smug, with an *I got my cake and ate it too* look.

If you see people using this pose, they have probably heard about it making one look intelligent and together. If they haven't and are naturally posing this way, well, they are calm and collected individuals. The pose does have a psychological effect and helps you to calm down and collect your thoughts.

1. Show generosity

This is a sweeping gesture to one side, made by stretching the arms out, fingers splayed, to mean, *all of it*. It can also mean *everything* in a different context.

"Just take your stuff and leave Jerry," Margo said disgustedly as she made a sweeping gesture toward the door.

"Just take it all; I don't use them," Sue told the charity fund as she swept her fingers across her collection of silk scarves.

1. Building up confidence

This is a hand gesture that shows size by changing the level of your palm. People use it to encourage and build confidence.

Speaking about investing in their company, Kyle held his hand at waist level and said, "So, you start with your base investment of a thousand dollars, and watch it grow. And by the end of one year, you are looking at 200% growth!" he said, raising his hand to shoulder level.

1. The grand motion

Have you seen people stand up, spread their arms out, and turn their palms out to face their audience? This hand cue signifies the person is being generous, noble, kind, or lenient; it's a grand gesture that showcases the person as being magnanimous.

Spreading out his hands, Frank told his friend Seth that offering him a job was the least he could do as payback for all the help he (Frank) received from Seth.

1. The inclusive gesture

If you need to make the other person feel confident, and you're rambling on about a specific subject, you can use the inclusive gesture to draw them in and make them a part of your conversation.

This is a simple gesture, where you stand close to the other person and extend your open hands toward them (as though you're pointing). Don't point with your finger, though, as pointing can be seen as aggressive or demanding at times.

1. The *me* gesture

This is a pretty simple hand gesture where you use both hands to point toward your chest, indicating yourself. People use this gesture to verify credibility, draw attention to themselves, and display sincerity.

"I myself have used the product and find it works excellently," Alex reiterated, pointing his hands to himself.

Let Your Fingers do the Talking

Since our fingers are attached to our hands (no kidding), there is not much communication reserved for just the fingers, but I will touch on some important factors here.

Listening to Fingers

Observe a person's fingers, and they will tell you about their mood, thoughts, and feelings since fingers often reflect what's going on in our minds.

- Tension—someone sitting with their fingers pressed together or even balled up into a fist is experiencing anxiety, panic, or stress.
- A relaxed state or personality—fingers spread out signals comfort.
- The conundrum—this is what I label finger-pointing. It's a rather sensitive body language, sometimes rude and sometimes necessary. Pointing at people, especially pointing aggressively, should be avoided. It's an imposing, authoritative pose, often used to talk down someone.

Sometimes, however, pointing becomes necessary, such as when you need to point out something, or give directions; therefore, make sure you understand the context of the situation before you judge a pointer.

- The threat—people who cannot accept your rebuttal or rejection of their suggestions, arguments, etc., or those who wish to threaten, will use this pose, which resembles a gun where the index finger is pointed, and others are folded, while the hand is held in a slanted position, and the arm outstretched.
- The insult—well, if you've got someone giving you the "finger," only the middle finger up and palm turned back, it means just one thing. No exceptions here.
- Boredom—drumming or tapping one's fingers is a sure sign of boredom or impatience. It's a self-

soothing action that both relieves and highlights one's displeasure or lack of enthusiasm.

- Rudeness—using the thumb to point is considered rude in just about every culture and should therefore be avoided.
- The "all-good," "okay" gesture—the thumbs up is a positive sign in the US and most Western nations. However, it can be the opposite in the Middle East, South America, Greece, Afghanistan, and some other nations where it's considered just as offensive as the middle finger—meaning "sit on it." Therefore, this is a gesture I generally avoid using when traveling.

As you now know, arms, hands, and fingers speak volumes! Besides learning to read their body language, you can use these body parts to enhance, influence, and expand your verbal conversations. When used in the correct context, arm, hand, and finger gestures can help influence your audience in a very effective manner.

Practice makes perfect, especially if you are not used to non-verbal communication using your upper body limbs. The good old mirror is the perfect tool for fine-tuning your arm, hand, and finger gestures. Aim to make them as smooth and natural as possible to create the right impact.

Next, let's move on to the most obvious section of a person's body—the face. Deciphering eye movements, head gestures, and smiles is all very interesting and intuitive.

Dear Reader,

We appreciate your support in buying this book! I am dedicated to providing quality books that help my fellow introvert's lives, and any positive feedback is vital to that.

If you find this book helpful, would you please take a brief moment to let others know your valuable opinion by snapping on the QR code below or by leaving a review on Amazon here. From my family to yours, thank you!

5

IT'S ALL IN THE HEAD

I believe every person has a story that comes out from the way they talk, their opinion, their mindset and their body language. —Diljit Dosanjh

Aaron had been dating Alexa for over a year and he planned to ask her to move in with him. However, he was not 100% sure about Alexa's feelings for him. There was always that one nagging feeling that left him in doubt. So, he decided to put his girlfriend's affections to the body language test.

The next time they went out for dinner, Aaron opened up a very purposeful conversation.

"My friend Jeremy is getting married next month. He finally asked Astrid, and she said yes," he told Alexa.

"Oh, good for him," Alexa said, diverting her attention to her salad. She did not look up at Aaron.

"Alexa, don't you think that once you find true love, it's best to make that relationship more permanent?"

"I guess it is," Alexa said, shrugging her shoulders.

"Well, I guess you and I are pretty close to taking our relationship to the next level," Aaron said, looking deeply at Alexa.

Alexa did not raise her head. She took a sip of her water stalling for time, "hmm, I guess" she faltered, still not looking at Aaron. She ran her fingers through her hair, laughed nervously and looked through hooded eyes at Aaron.

"Do you think we stand a chance to make our relationship work long term?" Aaron took the chance asking this question because alarm bells were now going off in his head. All the signs Alexa was giving him were negative.

"I guess we do, yes!" Alexa smiled, and as she said this, she unconsciously nodded her head in a classic *no* gesture.

Well, Aaron got his answer—not in the positive, as he had hoped. But he has moved on and found a more truthful and loving partner. Turns out Alexa had fallen out of love with him and simply could not find a way to let him know. But luckily for Aaron, her body language conveyed the message loud and clear.

Of all the body language you learned thus far, the head plays the biggest role, because it's the part that is most exposed and most watched. Your eyes are like windows to your soul, and your head can say a lot about your thoughts and moods through simple nods, tilts, and shakes. The slight curve of your mouth, your smile, your frown—they all offer microscopic reactions that, when caught by the discerning eye, can be deciphered to *see* what you're truly thinking.

Heads Up! —What Are They Thinking?

Our heads go through several actions during the course of a day, and if we were to put all those gestures together, we would look as though our necks were springs.

From nodding to turning and rotating, to even pointing,

heads perform a range of tasks. They never stop talking, even when our lips are sealed shut.

Here are some classic head gestures and their meanings.

Raising the Head

Raising a lowered head can have several meanings. When the person who is looking down at their hands with great interest, as when reading a book or flicking through their phone, suddenly raises their head and looks at you, it's a signal that you caught their attention. The reasons for their reaction can vary, so let's explore them below.

1. The *Huh?* look. This means the person suddenly wants to know what you meant.

Example: When Mavis announced to Joe that she was quitting her job, he closed his laptop and looked up at her with puzzled amazement.

1. It can also be a reaction to a surprising and shocking statement. When coupled with raised eyebrows, it sometimes indicates curiosity and interest.

Example: "Have you ever gone skinny dipping in winter?" Blake asked his date, who put down her fork to look at him with one raised eyebrow.

1. Imagining or visualizing. A person trying to envision something in their heads may suddenly look up and squint their eyes.

Example: Mary stopped writing her story, squinted her eyes, and looked up at the sky through her window, trying to imagine a melodramatic ending to the tale she was telling.

1. Boredom is another sign indicated by a head being raised to look upward.

Example: As Edgar described his job sorting mail at the post office, his young nephew sighed, raised his head, and stared at the lampshade hanging from the ceiling.

Lowering the Head

The main instinct behind lowering our heads is protection. Recall those airline drills where you are told to lower your head and hug the pillow in case of an emergency.

Here are some other negative reasons behind our instinctive reactions for head lowering.

- Submission and fear. Lowering the head and eyes is a sign of compliance brought on by fear or nervousness. It can also be a mark of respect and love.

In some cultures, elders are shown respect and love by younger people who bow their heads or lower their eyes in their presence.

A person who fears another person will avoid looking them in the eye, believing that avoiding eye contact will make them less noticeable. Eye contact is interactive and initiates cooperation, which is the last thing a nervous person wants to encourage. Lowering the head and diverting the eyes away from someone helps maintain privacy. We are preventing the other person from seeing too much.

Our eyes often mirror our true feelings, thoughts, and emotions, which is why insecure, or dishonest people avoid making direct eye contact. Since we cannot close our eyes when talking, we lower our heads to hide them.

- Lethargy. Feeling sluggish or depressed can be reflected through a lowered head, which means the person feels helpless. They may be dealing with a mental health problem, or they may be exhausted.
- Flirtation. Women often use this gesture as a coy way of gaining attention. The head is slightly bent, while the eyes look up at the person in an endearing manner.
- Distrust. Lowering the head while looking at the other person is meant to say, *I don't trust you*. They are not prepared to relax 100% in the other person's company.
- Secret signal to say *okay* or *no*. Let's say you are at a meeting ready to sign a very lucrative deal with another party. You notice your business partner give a small nod to their colleague–a very slight nod, that goes almost unnoticed as their head bends ever so slightly. This is a secret nod to say *okay*. It can also work as a *no*, where a slight shake of the head from either side is interpreted by the receiver to mean *no, don't do it*.

The Head Tilt

Tilting the head is attractive and makes you noticeable, but which way your head should tilt to ensure your success depends on your gender.

The Look of Pride and So Much More

This is a universal sign of power and self-confidence. A head tilted upward is a positive sign. It shows you are strong, proud, and confident. People look up to those who have a natural upward head tilt.

The signal is pretty literal, too; women find the facial features of men who tilt their heads upward more attractive. Why? It makes them look taller and dominant (Windhager et al., 2011). Times may have changed, but our genes still carry blueprints from when our hunter-gatherer ancestors defined genders by strength. It's a rule of the animal world—the alpha male rules.

A head tilting up and slightly to the side signals interest as well as honesty. If someone is sending you this signal, it means they find your conversation engaging. They are concentrating and thinking about what you have to say.

Tilting your head up to look at someone fills us with awe, or hope–sort of like the time when as a kid, you looked up at your parents (literally, and as a mark of respect). We experience this same sense of authority and confidence when we tilt our heads up at someone.

The Look of Modesty

Women who tilt their heads down, lowering their eyelids, appear more demure and coy, thus increasing their attractiveness. Indeed, as studies show, stereotypical gender heights do matter when it comes to the laws of subconscious attraction (Vaca et al., 2021).

To make these poses work in your favor, practice. Use a mirror to perfect your head tilt, whether you are a man or a woman. Head tilting is thought to increase your chances of forming a positive connection and makes you look more endearing.

The Sudden Tilt Back

This is the *whaaat* gesture that shows surprise. If someone suddenly tilts their head right back, their eyebrows shoot up, and their eyes widen, it's a sure sign of shock.

One may follow the same gesture with a facepalm or slap to the side of the head, indicating they are overwhelmed, shocked, or surprised.

A sudden double take will also indicate shock, a sudden interest in what you said, or disbelief, as when a person exclaims, "What did you just say?!" This is a kind of jerky head movement that makes them look at you and then look away twice, in quick succession.

The Nod

A head nod indicates a *yes, I agree,* as well as *yes, I am listening, go ahead.*

- If you notice someone nodding their head vigorously, it probably means, *yes, yes, I see. Now can I have a turn to speak?*

Vigorous nodding means the other person has a reciprocal comment on what's being discussed and is dying to get it out.

- A head nod means *yes* just about every time unless the person is not being truthful. So how do you tell if a "yes! That's a wonderful idea" is really an enthusiastic reply or not?

You watch for the microexpressions, such as pursued lips, that follow a "yes" statement but that actually signal a lie. Lips that are pulled in indicate the other person is frustrated or disapproves of what's going on or being discussed. The slight smirk is another sign that someone is being condescending while nodding "yes."' Watch for the slight pull down of one side of the mouth–a slight smirk that lasts a microsecond.

- The *yes* nod to a *no*. Someone telling a fib and answering in the negative when a *yes* would be an honest answer will subconsciously come clean. They will say, "no!" but their heads will nod a *yes.* Watch for this automatic expression, and you will be able to confirm your suspicions if you feel something is off.

- Finally, here's how to use the simple head nod to manipulate. Let's say you need someone to agree with you. You give them your pitch and then nod your head to say *yes*. This subtle gesture invites the other person to answer in the positive too. It's not black magic–simply the magic of body language.

Here are some examples:

"Don't you agree that increasing the advertising budget will help gain more exposure for the brand?" This is said while nodding *yes*.

"Hey Suzie, wouldn't it be a great idea to ask Mark over for dinner?" Jeff asked as he nodded his head in a *yes*. Looking at him, Suzie couldn't help but reciprocate the nod that said *yes!*

The Recharge

This is a common gesture we often see in movies where the overly confident sheriff places his feet on his desk and leans back, putting his hands behind his head for his elbows to flare out. He then asks the bully millionaire to "Take a hike, mister!"

This is a confidence-boosting pose and non-verbal form of communication that says, *I'm the boss, watch out*. It's also called the cobra pose because a cobra raises its hood to intimidate and threaten enemies. Use this pose, like the power pose we discussed in Chapter 2, to boost your confidence. It has a knack for relieving nervousness and low confidence.

The Introvert's Tool

What would you do if you are not great at conversation? Here's this person who can simply talk non-stop and keep your conversation flowing (even though it's mostly one-sided). All you have to do is nod or add a one-syllable answer, and they continue the conversation. Eazy peazy, right? Well, here's a trick to make them keep talking. You nod three times in quick succession.

What you do is nod three times vigorously as soon as there

is a pause in the conversation, and you want them to keep talk-ing. The non-verbal cue works almost every time and will get the other person to engage in the conversation for another couple of minutes.

Hair Twirling, Pulling, and Ruffling

We recognize hair twirling as a classic flirtatious pose. A woman who twirls a lock of her hair, raises her head to expose her neck and looks your way is sending you a strong signal to say she is attracted to you. Tossing the head, flicking the hair back, and exposing more of the neck work together to say, *hey, I think you're cute; look at me!*

Hair is a good indicator of mood; for example, a disheveled head may indicate stress, depression, or simply a lack of self-motivation and self-care.

- If there is no hair twirling, and the man or woman is running their hands through their hair, or pulling at it, it's possibly a sign of stress or anxiety, and playing with their hair is a self-soothing gesture.
- Ruffling one's hair can indicate the person is feeling uncomfortable, perhaps due to the situation or the question. Some people use this gesture to indicate they are thinking and stalling for time.
- Women often play with their hair as a self-soothing gesture. Lifting hair at the back of the neck in the act of cooling down or raising their hair as they run their hands through their hair, indicates various feelings, such as stress, insecurity, shyness, or feeling flustered. Use your intuition to gauge the context of the situation before you make a judgment call.

Pointing With the Head

We learned earlier about pointing feet at someone who holds everyone's attention; well, the head acts in a similar manner. People seated at a meeting will often be seen pointing their heads, chins very slightly up, at the most powerful person in the room. You can use this cue to quickly figure out who is popular, who holds authority, etc., in a group you have just joined; a majority of people will be head-pointing at this person.

Head-Propping and Tapping

A person who is exhausted will sometimes hold their head in their hands. They may also tap their forehead to indicate stress. Sometimes, tapping can also indicate low self-esteem, in an, *I'm stupid* kind of gesture.

The Unmoving Head

What does it mean when the head does not move at all?

This is a show of power, as the still head lets the person fix everyone with a steely gaze. It says, *I'm in charge, I see you, now pay attention.* Keeping the head still is a sign of deep concentration. Think of the boss who is surveying his employees, or someone staring at an activity trying to gauge the situation.

Facing Feelings, Thoughts, and Emotions

Your face can speak a thousand words—silently. The lips, eyes, nose, and ears–all pitch in to make body language a trusted tool for revealing what you or the other person is thinking or feeling. The face is where you can catch those microexpressions–the slight changes that cross a person's features, however fleetingly, to reveal their true thoughts and emotions.

Learning to fine-tune your microexpression reading skills will certainly enhance your body language reading expertise. Facial expressions are elusive because they can change depending on both how you feel and how others react to you.

Why Are Microexpressions Important?

Microexpressions cannot lie, which makes them one of the most accurate tools for reading people. Faking them is tough because they are automatic reflexes. A microexpression will last from around 0.2 to 0.5 seconds (Shen et al., 2012), so you need to be sharp and fine-tune your microexpression reading skills through practice.

Charles Darwin was the first to explore and confirm that emotional micro-expressions are universal, which means that no matter where you are, even in the midst of a remote African tribe, facial expressions for standard emotions–anger, fear, anxiety, surprise, etc.–are the same. While it's tough to manipulate microexpressions, it's possible to misread them.

Take contempt, for example. It's one of the most misinterpreted micro-expressions because it's fleeting and often looks like boredom or even feelings of joy. No matter how well you think you can read facial expressions, it's possible to make a mistake; hence, it's important to understand how facial features work together to display a certain emotion in less than a second.

Most Common Microexpressions

An interesting phenomenon with emotions is how you automatically mirror them. Can you recall a time your face changed to look exactly like the face your friend/family member was pulling when they saw something fearful?

This is because the amygdala, the part of your brain that responds with a fight or flight reaction, is sensitive to emotions that evoke fear, hurt, shock, etc. Mirroring is how your senses respond and prepare for an imminent threat.

1. Disgust

One of the easiest microexpressions to catch, the look of disgust on a person's face is not very flattering.

Microexpressions to watch out for:

- eyes narrow to help focus on that one point that's making them feel disgusted.
- the upper lip goes up, and the front row of teeth may be revealed, almost like a snarl.
- the cheeks rise, and the nose scrunches up.

Not the prettiest sight, but it should be avoided if you don't fancy looking unattractive—even for a split second.

1. Fear

Eyebrows that scoot up are clear signs of distress, and so when fear is reflected, it looks a lot like a shock.

Microexpressions to watch out for:

- Eyes open wide; it's an auto reflex to help us see better by increasing our visual field. The upper whites of the eyes, not the lower, become visible. Likewise, the upper lid rises while the lower eyelid looks scrunched up.
- The mouth opens in readiness for a scream if necessary—help! It's also a reflex to help take in more oxygen in case you need to outrun a threat.
- The eyebrows shoot up.
- The forehead wrinkles can be seen in the middle area.

1. Surprise

Curved eyebrows are pretty basic when it comes to identifying surprise on someone's face.

- The pupils appear to float in the middle of the eyes as whites become visible both top and bottom.

- The mouth goes slack and drops open but minus
  any tension.

The reason the eyebrows curve up and eyes open wide is often a display of honesty. You will notice this cue among people who get offended at being wrongly accused. This gesture is also a sign of attraction, and if you notice your date flashes an arched brow, and wide eyes look at you, it means they think you're cool.

1. Anger

Anger is a social taboo in most instances, and people often try to disguise this emotion. Therefore, you need to be observant to catch the microexpressions that give away this emotion. Microexpressions to watch out for:

- A quick downward pull of the eyebrows forms a V.
- Vertical lines, often in the form of an eleven (11),
  appear between the brows as they pull close to form
  the V.
- The lips compress, sometimes, the edges get pulled
  down, while the lower lip is more scrunched.
- The jaw clenches and becomes prominent.
- The nostrils flare.
- The eyes become slits and will look hard and stare.

We are sensitive to emotions like anger, for fear of offending, or getting hurt physically, and therefore are naturally more observant of these microexpressions.

1. Sadness

A sad face is not easy to detect, although it's also an

emotion we are sensitive to for fear of offending or causing worry.

Microexpressions to watch out for:

- The eyebrows are pulled down at the outer edges as the inner edges rise up, forming an upside-down V.
- The jaw juts out, and lower lip pouts, while the outer corners of the mouth are pulled down. Children have perfected this signal.
- The inner corner of the eyelids go up, and the outer corners are pulled down.

Microexpressions for sadness last much longer than others and become easier to detect. Yet not every sad face denotes sadness, as some people have naturally looked at sad faces, much like the resting bitch face (RBF).

I. Happiness

Happiness is a refreshing microexpression that we can't help mirroring. How many times have you grinned for no reason simply because the other person was smiling like crazy?

Microexpressions to watch out for:

- Drain-like lines form from the outer corner of the nose to meet the corner of the mouth.
- The mouth is turned up, and teeth become visible, or sometimes the lips are stretched up in a large U.
- The eyes scrunch up, and the crow's feet appear at the outer edges.
- The cheeks rise up.

An important cue to look for is a smile that reaches the eyes. This happens when the eye muscles are used, and the bottom half of the eyes form an upward curve, kind of like an upside-down smile. Any smile that does not reach the eyes is forced or fake.

1. Hate or Contempt

This one can be misinterpreted as it denotes a curled-up mouth. The rest of the face remains neutral, and this microexpression is fleeting.

Last but not least, watch out for the mouth that curls up on one side. This could mean the person considers themselves superior. You are wrong, and they are right. It's a very negative emotion that often spells trouble. If faced with this microexpression, use it as a cue to begin some damage control before it's too late—once you identify the reason behind the contemptuous look, of course.

These microexpressions need to be studied, and practice makes perfect. Identifying the circumstance behind the signals is important for a proper prediction of what triggers the emotion.

Eyes That Mirror the Soul

When talking to someone, we often look into their eyes for a better understanding of what they are feeling, especially if we are discussing an issue with serious emotional implications. And emotions do indeed cross the eyes, even for a fleeting second, so you must be sharp enough to catch them.

Microexpressions to watch out for:

Blinking

- Rapid blinks can signal distress, shock, nervousness, or dishonesty; being overwhelmed and unable to speak fluently; strong sexual arousal or attraction.

They could also happen due to bright lights, so be observant.

- If someone blinks very little, it indicates they are trying their best to get their emotions under control or to conceal them.
- Eye batting is a type of fluttery blinking that is used to make a person look more alluring when flirting.

Staring

- Eyes that stare signal suppressed anger or agitation that's building up.
- Quiet disbelief, as well as discomfort, caused staring.
- The liars stare. We often associate looking away and breaking eye contact when talking as a liar trait, which is true. However, some liars will maintain eye contact throughout the lie, and keep staring after to catch a signal in your face that the lie was accepted.
- The creepy stare can take place when men are on a date, find the woman fascinating, and forget to break eye contact, when talking, to avoid making the other person feel uncomfortable. If you face this, go ahead and crack a joke, or find an excuse to look away.
- Winks are often used as an icebreaker, to avoid too much staring. They also indicate friendliness as well as attraction. Decide on the context of the situation.

Dilated Pupils

- Dilated eyes signal interest in something or even arousal. The larger the interest, the wider the dilation.
- Anger causes pupil dilation.
- It's also a response to a lack of light.

Body Language of the Eyes

Eye movement can signal several emotions, but here are the most common cues to watch out for.

Cast Down Eyes

Similar to the downward head tilt, eyes that look down denote submission or respect. This is a norm in Southeast Asian nations, China, Japan, etc., where it's customary to respect elders and superiors by showing submission in the form of a bent head and downcast eyes.

If someone suddenly looks down during a conversation, it can mean the following:

- They're feeling uncomfortable due to what was just said.
- They're feeling guilt or insecurity.
- They are thinking about a question you asked them. In a group discussion, some people look down to ponder what was said.

Eyes That Swivel from Left to Right

A person who looks from the corner of their eyes silently is indicating they have doubts, are suspicious, are reluctant to commit, or are feeling contemptuous. If this gesture is followed by a wrinkled brow, it means they don't quite agree and need further clarification.

This gesture can also indicate a person is eavesdropping or silently watching an activity they are not a part of; their eyes will shift to the corner where the dialogue or activity is taking place. This happens, minus any head movement, to remain unnoticed.

Looking sideways is also a signal to say they are pondering, processing what was discovered, or thinking of an answer.

Looking sideways while stating something may also signal dishonesty. However, to make an accurate judgment, you need to match this cue with other facial and body language cues to confirm the person is telling a lie.

Looking Up

A person who has been asked a question will often look up, as a signal they are thinking. It can also convey exasperation.

"Darn it, I forgot to buy milk again!" said Mom as she looked up in annoyance.

Tilted Head and Sideways Glance

This is the cue for *Yeah, right! I don't think so.*

If someone you are talking to suddenly gives you a sideways head tilt and glances from the side of their eyes, they are in disbelief.

If they slightly nod in a direction and then move their pupils to the corner of their eyes in a sort of point, they are trying to draw your attention to a person or incident taking place in that direction. Sometimes people simply point with their eyes without moving their head to try and get the attention of the talker to say, *hey, look over there.*

The Glazed Look

If you have been talking for too long, and the other person suddenly gets a faraway look in their eyes, making them appear well, glazed over, it's a sure sign of boredom and loss of interest. Move on, change the topic, or let them walk away to newer and better conversations.

Body Language of the Lips

We already covered the movement of lips in reaction to various emotions. Here are a few more common gestures that give away secret thoughts and feelings.

Puckered Lips

They say *I'm ready to be kissed*, symbolizing desire. This is true, especially if the person is touching their lips while talking and looking at your lips.

Sucked in Lips

This gesture looks as though the person has swallowed

their lips because they are no longer visible. It's a cue to say they are holding back their words because they are literally sealing their mouth shut to prevent themselves from speaking. The gesture may be adopted by someone who has to deliver bad news and is reluctant to do so, thus buying time. Or the person is getting ready to tell a lie.

Sealed Flat

Pressing the lips together to form a straight line is called a lip press. This happens when someone is upset and does not agree with what's being said. It's a safety mechanism to stop saying something that will sound harsh. The gesture also says they are patiently waiting their turn to speak.

Rolling, Moving, and Chewing On Lips

This is a subconscious movement. Someone who is listening in on a conversation may start moving their lips in the shape of words, ever so subtly that it's hard to catch. But it does happen and means they are thinking of what to say.

Chewing on lips indicates someone is thinking, is anxious, or is nervous. Lip rolling happens when a person feels uncomfortable or is at a loss for words, and it also occurs unconsciously among women when they try to spread out their lipstick evenly.

Covering the Lip

If the top lip overlaps the bottom lip, which the person is biting, it indicates anxiety, in most cases brought on by the act of lying.

If the bottom lip is pulled over the top lip, it means the person is uncertain about something. Or they are in disagreement and are pouting. (Yes, even adults pout, but often unconsciously).

Both Lips Pressed Out

When people press both lips together and then push them out, they are most likely doubtful. Additionally, tapping a finger against those protruding lips says, *hmm, I'm thinking about it.*

Lips that look relaxed say the owner is feeling laidback, too, with no inner turmoil or thoughts to activate their facial expressions.

Body Language of the Nose

The nose knows! There is no doubt about what these gestures mean. Let's sniff them out!

The Discreet Nose Touch

This is a sneaky gesture, with dishonest connotations.

Discreetly touching the nose signals the person means the opposite of what they are saying because they are being dishonest. It's also a silent cry for help that says, *all is not right*, or a sign that they don't agree with you.

Someone who secretly touches their nose is also faking interest and may not be as happy or enthusiastic to see you or be in your company. Sounds shocking? Well, the nose knows!

How do people sneak in a nose touch?

- While they're swatting at a fly that's hovering around, they take a quick swipe at the nose.
- While talking, they quickly swipe at the nose with the index finger.
- They hold a fist under the chin like a prop that also slightly touches the nose.
- They use the forearm to swipe at the nose.

The difference between these stealthy attempts to touch the nose and openly touching the nose is the dishonesty that's running through someone's mind at that moment.

"Love your idea of meeting up for a movie on Saturday! Just let me check my schedule and let you know," Alison told Hans while taking a quick swipe at her nose as though chasing away a fly. She was already thinking about an excuse to avoid the proposed date.

Touching, Scratching, or Rubbing

Apart from sneaking a touch of the nose, people openly touch, rub, and scratch at their noses. Such negative gestures suggest the person is nervous, anxious, unsure, unconvinced, or stressed out. Stress or uncomfortable situations may cause the heart to beat faster and, thus, the nose to itch or tingle due to elevated breathing as blood is being pumped faster.

The Warning, Side-Nose Touch

Discreetly touching the side of the nose with the index finger is a warning signal in some cultures. If someone does this, they may be telling you to watch out for danger from unscrupulous people close by.

It's also a signal to say, *this is a secret; keep it to yourself.* The gesture is often accompanied by raised eyebrows and a slight knowing nod. It's often adopted once someone has disclosed private information to you.

Pinching the Bridge of the Nose

We often associate this action with stress, such as when someone takes off their reading glasses and pinches the bridge of their nose with their thumb and index finger. The action signals deep thinking, frustrations, or worry.

The Nose Cover

A shocking, surprising, overwhelming, fearful, or sad event makes people cover their noses and part of their forehead with cupped hands. It's a kind of self-soothing gesture, kind of like breathing into a paper bag to regulate our heartbeat. It's also an instinct to muffle the sound of increased breathing that can be brought on by sudden fear.

These little nosey insights are great cues to determining the success of a conversation, as well as to manipulating the unconscious messages you may be sending to other people.

An Earful of Body Language

The ears may not be the most likely candidate, when it comes to body language, because, most of the time, they just sit there on either side of your head—listening and not talking.

But, you *can* read ears through simple observation, such as color change and ear touching.

Ears are susceptible to body temperature fluctuations, not so much in Asian people, but the ears of fair-skinned people whose skin color is sensitive to heat fluctuations will talk quite a bit.

Blue or Red

Extreme cold can cause ears to turn blue, which is a straightforward signal. Red ears that are accompanied by a sweaty brow and heavy breathing indicate physical exertion, such as after a bout of running, or exercise.

Other Causes for Red Ear

Attraction: Passion and strong sexual arousal will make a person's ears appear reddened. And now you know an embarrassing little secret.

Anger: The tips of the ears turn red following a sudden rush of blood to the ears caused by an increased heart rate. The anger is not always easy to gauge because, most of the time, the tips of the ears are hidden by hair.

Stress: Similar to how someone reacts to anger, their ears turn red when they person is stressed. You can determine the trigger by looking for other facial expressions that confirm its stress or anger.

Embarrassment: The ears turn red as the person blushes, making it easy to read this cue.

The Cues

Similar to touching the nose to signal danger, people will use non-verbal signals to indicate their hearing abilities.

- Cupping the hand to the ear and turning the head so the ear faces you is a signal to say, *I can't hear you speak up.*
- Pointing or tapping at the ear is also a signal to say, *you are not audible.*

These gestures are often used in noisy areas and are universal signals to say *cannot hear*.

- Placing a hand over one ear, or covering both ears, says, *I don't want to listen to you.* or *stop talking; I've heard enough!*
- Placing both hands on the ears and then pulling them apart is how a deaf person will indicate they cannot hear.

Now that we have covered every part of your body that speaks silently, it's time to start practicing your newfound skills. The next chapter offers an added bonus that will sharpen your body language reading skills.

Let's look at thin-slicing and develop the ability to gauge a room full of people through a few sweeping glances! Sounds awesome? Let's get started.

6

THIN SLICES OF LIFE

There can be as much value in the blink of an eye as in months of rational analysis. —Malcolm Gladwell

E rrol walked into the boardroom and sat down with his team. They were pitching to market a big account and had a whole impressive presentation lined up. In walked the CEO and his manager, who smiled hello, but to Errol they both looked pressed for time and impatient. Looking at his team, he realized they were geared for a long and impressive pitch, but looking at the CEO and his manager, he made a split-second decision.

Cutting out the opening proposal, Errol presented the final section of the pitch, where monetary gains and market share were mentioned.

"This is the result we offer you, and how we plan to take you there is in the rest of the pitch. If you are interested, we can email you our full proposal or reschedule to a day when you have a few hours to spare."

Suffice to say, Errol's quick interpretation of the situation and five-minute decision to change their approach were correct. The CEO was in a rush due to a personal reason that had cropped up. Presenting the final slides was a smart move, and they won the account, with a reschedule to go over the details. Had Errol asked his team to make the full presentation, chances are the CEO would have left halfway, undecided, with a rain check to continue the rest of the pitch.

What Is Thin-Slicing?

Get that image of sliced bread out of your head! That's not the type of thin slice under discussion here.

Malcolm Gladwell, whose apt quote sits at the top of this chapter, expounds on the theory of thin-slicing; he calls it *thinking without thinking* in his book *Blink,* and in reality, it is. Thin-slicing will help you to walk into a room and assess the crowd there by reading body language and considering the context of the situation.

Thin-slicing is what we call sudden decisions made on a quick analysis of a situation or person, in as little as five minutes. It does not have to be a calculated evaluation like the one I mentioned above. Experiencing a sudden emotional reaction, based on a deduction from past events, is also how thin-slicing works.

Here's an example:

When Jasper didn't show up for work by 9 a.m. on Monday, Harold the boss was irritated, assuming that once more Jasper had decided to take a Monday off.

Harold was thin-slicing and basing his decision on Jasper's past behavior. His emotional reaction was tied to the conclusion drawn through thin-slicing. It's kind of like jumping to a judgment based on a perception or set of past events.

Thin-slicing is not the best type of analysis for important decisions because all of the facts and data are not taken into consideration. You are skimming the surface to arrive at a quick decision. Therefore, I find that the thin-slicing strategy works best in certain situations, such as when you need to gauge a room full of people and assess their attitudes and emotions in order to know who to talk to and who to avoid; as such, thin-slicing is a valuable tool if you are an introvert.

First Impressions and Thin-Slicing Methods

Whether it's love at first sight or that old adage that says, *first impressions never lie*, a good portion of our everyday choices are based on split-second decisions.

How often have you judged the likeability of a person by simply saying "hello," and then thinking, *what a nice person*, or *I don't like her*.

The Science Behind Thin-Slicing

Your first impression judgment of someone may not be all that wrong. Experiments prove that all we need are a few seconds to assess a person's personality (Miller et al., 2004). Establishing baseline analysis for gauging a person's trustworthiness is crucial to forming quick assessments, which means that microexpressions and how well we pick up on them play a part in influencing our decisions.

What Are the Main Personality Traits on Which We Rate Others?

We rate ourselves as well as others by identifying the main personality traits from among the following five:

- Intellect, which is mainly assessed on a cultural basis.
- Responsibility, which is gauging how conscientious a person is.
- Sociable quality, which refers to the level of extroversion.
- Being agreeable, which represents a person's good nature.

- Emotional stability, which denotes levels of calmness.

Extroversion and sociability standards are the most noticeable characteristics on which we can base pretty accurate assessments of other people.

Parameters on Which We Form First Impressions

Self-evaluations based on these characteristics are not as accurate as when we judge the other person—there is too much bias involved. Quite often, our perception of ourselves can sometimes be over- or under-rated. However, there is no bias when it comes to judging the personality of the other person based on the above characteristics.

First impressions are often gauged not on the person's entire character but on a specific aspect that may be important at the time.

For example, if you are interviewing a host of nannies to take care of your child, you would focus more on their intellect, emotional stability, and responsibility than other characteristics.

How accurate are first impressions?

Parameters that define how successfully a first impression is formed are based on cultural differences; for instance, how Asians socialize may be different from how people in the West socialize; therefore, the baseline on which we judge their socializing skills will be different. The final decision also depends on the person judging and how much of a rapport they have built with the person.

So yes, first impressions are not 100% accurate. There are times that first impressions can turn out to be horribly wrong. An extrovert psychopath with a pleasant personality is hard to identify and can often fool people. The person you thought was empathetic may be impatient. It takes time to really delve deep into a person's personality.

The two most accurate tools for forming a successful first impression of someone are judging first impressions within one's culture, which is the same as judging body language, and fine-tuning your body language reading skills.

The Connection Between Thin-Slicing and Body Language

Connecting your judgment of the person's character with accurate body language signals will help form the most accurate first impression. Here are some basic questions you can ask yourself before you make that final decision—minus any bias. Look for microexpressions and other non-verbal cues that will help back up your thin-slicing observations to form a mostly accurate judgment of character.

- Does the person agree with what's being discussed?
- Does their body language evoke a controlling nature?
- Are their actions in line with those of responsible people you know?
- Are they acting normal, given the situation?
- Are they showing traits of introversion or extroversion?

Thin-slicing certainly has its benefits, especially when you need a confidence boost at a social gathering, business meeting, etc. Couple the rules for thin slicing with your newly found body language reading cues, and you may not be too far off from making accurate first impression judgments.

Next, let's move on to a topic that makes body language a powerful tool—detecting lies and dishonesty.

7

DETECTING LIES AND DECEPTION

I don't mind being called a liar. I am. I am a marvelous liar. But I hate being called a liar when I´m telling the perfect truth. —Patrick Rothfuss

"Hey man, it's good to see you, I've been meaning to call you for so long!" Jack, my neighbor, called out as I opened the door to his knocking. Jack stepped in, sat down, made himself comfortable, and surveyed my apartment.

"I've got a proposition for you, a pretty lucrative deal, that requires a minimum contribution. I've got a friend hounding me to cut them in on the deal, but I thought you deserved first shot," Jack said, giving his nose a small swipe, and looking down at his phone as he said the last sentence.

"What do you say? Are you interested? Marty in 2B is pretty eager to get in on the deal," Jack said while automatically shaking his head in a *no* signal.

I took a deep breath before saying, "Oh, I'm sorry Jack, but I'm not in a position to invest in anything right now." Suffice to say, I avoided any kind of commitment and sent Jack off to look for a new victim.

Apart from Jack's reputation as a scammer, I was alerted to his lies by all the negative body language the man was displaying: eyes that looked away, the nose touching, and even the way he shifted his head in a *no* gesture when he meant a *yes*.

Uncovering the Truth About Lying and How It Affects the Body

Everyone lies at some point of their lives. In fact, on average, we may lie about one to four times a day. A majority admit to inconsequential lying where their lies have no damaging impact (Verigin et al., 2019). Telling someone their cooking tastes good when it's not, building self-confidence with a small white lie, etc. are examples of how we lie for the greater good.

Most people who consider themselves to be successful liars will attempt to adjust their non-verbal cues to conceal the dishonesty. However, getting the best of those automatic microexpressions is tough. That's where you can step in to detect the deceit.

Pathological liars will tell around ten lies a day and may be smart enough to manipulate their body language to match the lie. But what they can't escape are the physical consequences of a dishonest lifestyle—that's right, lying is bad for your health!

The Health Implications of a Dishonest Lifestyle

Think about it: If you are not comfortable telling lies, the moment you do, you feel a sense of guilt, discomfort, and well, some self-loathing too. Even people who are regularly dishonest will experience a small degree of guilt. And although a pathological liar may not wallow in guilt, keeping up a dishonest lifestyle can be stressful. After all, lies do have a domino effect and require meticulous planning, acting, and keeping notes to keep up the charade of dishonesty. That's where the anxiety creeps in.

Lying leads to an increase in stress hormones, high blood pressure, elevated heart rate, and vasoconstriction, which means your blood vessels narrow.

Vasoconstriction can take place due to emotional stress (such as maintaining and living with lies) that triggers a nervous reaction within the brain, causing a lesser flow of blood to the heart. This, in turn, causes the blood to thicken, resulting in constricted blood vessels and high blood pressure (Shah et al., 2019).

What are the implications of a lying lifestyle?

- Lost trust. A liar hurts the people they love. Lying causes irreversible damage at times because lost trust is hard to regain.
- Depression. Lying to hide emotional issues, stress, and anxiety don't make them go away. You are merely adding to the problems. This, in turn, increases anxiety and can lead to clinical depression.
- Self-loathing. Despite being a successful liar to others, you cannot deceive yourself. And the emotional stress you are burdened with when dealing with a deceitful lifestyle often leads to low self-esteem and even hating oneself.

However, this does not mean that all liars are dealing with heart ailments and stress. Some people do develop a tolerance, and their brains get comfortable with their devious way of life. Hence, they will continue to be dishonest, with no qualms. This lack of remorse makes society, as a whole, intolerable toward liars.

How to Spot a Liar Through Body Language

Throughout the book, we analyzed subtle cues and signals that help you to detect a lie or dishonest answer.

These signals, in combination with other microexpressions, make it easier to spot a liar.

Here are some examples:

- Tone that does not match the body language—a liar will adopt a higher tone of voice, while their body language remains calm.
- Sucking in the lips until they disappear, before speaking, suggests the person is preparing to lie.
- Vehemently denying any negative implications against them while working hard to make sure the allegations are diffused is another sign the person is trying to cover dishonesty.
- Fraudsters will expand their frame when sitting, interrupt others mid-sentence quite often, and use a lot of arm gestures.
- Covering the mouth is a sign the person is not telling you the whole story.
- Acting differently from one's baseline body language.
- Delaying a response to your question, or repeating the question, is a signal they are buying time to formulate an appropriate answer.
- The *I want to leave* non-verbal cues, such as feet pointing away, looking over your shoulder, averting eye contact, etc.
- Vague answers, such as *maybe* or *I don't know,* mean they are not telling the entire story.

Why Do People Lie?

We all lie, and unless we are pathological liars or deceitful people, we often tell a fib that benefits the other person. They are non-consequential lies told out of politeness or as a courtesy.

Here are some standard reasons that make people lie:

- as a favor to protect a friend, family member, co-worker, and sometimes a person you just met
- to avoid consequences, such as punishment or a scolding
- to protect ourselves when threatened

Example: "No, thank you, my husband is five minutes away," Mavis lied to the stranger who was offering her a lift from the station.

- to gain an advantage, by lying about your qualifications or work experience during a job interview
- to avoid socializing or an event you prefer to miss

Example: "Oh, sorry, I have to work the night shift next Saturday and won't make it to your party," Stephen lied.

- to look popular, fit in, or be noticed
- to avoid embarrassment, as when lying about exam results, one's job title, social status, etc.
- to control or wield power over someone by manipulating them, and not just for political reasons (which motivate dictators)

Example: "If you don't eat your greens, your insides will explode," a toxic parent might threaten their child.

Despite a person's well-concealed deception, being observant and sharp can help you to catch that flash microexpression, alerting you to what is really meant or going on. An interesting exercise I practiced to fine-tune my lie-detecting skills was to ask random questions of people I interacted with on a daily basis. I made sure the questions were mildly uncomfortable, just enough to make them want to gloss over the truth. This helped me to pick up on body language that contradicted their baseline behavior.

AFTERWORD

Congratulations on completing book two and, thus, your journey of mastering socializing and introversion. You are now armed with a set of skills that will empower you to overcome any reservations you may have over striking up a conversation and interacting with people.

The body language cues discussed in each chapter will open up a whole new avenue of communication for you. You are going to start seeing people in a new light. Body language is more evocative than words, and by being sensitive to each microexpression and physical gesture, you will *see* the true intention behind a person's words and actions, as well as your impact on them.

Remember that understanding the context of the situation is just as important as reading non-verbal signals correctly. Practice makes perfect, and you've got a whole smorgasbord of people out there to fine-tune your body language reading skills.

Good luck!

Leave a Review

I would love to read a positive review! Let me know your thoughts on book two by leaving a review on Amazon.

Oh, and watch out for more books to come in this series as we further investigate and fine-tune your social and communication skills!

P.S. If you enjoyed this book, please check out the rest of the series!

BIBLIOGRAPHY

Anthony, M. (2021, September 2). *25+ of the most insightful Malcolm Gladwell quotes*. Audible Blog. https://www.audible.com/blog/quotes-malcolm-gladwell

Bastiaansen, J. A. C. J., Thioux, M., & Keysers, C. (2009). Evidence for mirror systems in emotions. *Philosophical Transactions of the Royal Society B: Biological Sciences, 364*(1528), 2391–2404. https://doi.org/10.1098/rstb.2009.0058

Baxter, M. G., & Croxson, P. L. (2012). Facing the role of the amygdala in emotional information processing. *Proceedings of the National Academy of Sciences, 109*(52), 21180–21181. https://doi.org/10.1073/pnas.1219167110

Body language of the feet (Learn the secrets of the feet). (2021, December 10). Body Language Matters. https://bodylanguagematters.com/body-language-of-feet/

Bull, D. (n.d.). *Deborah Bull quotes*. BrainyQuote. Retrieved January 12, 2023, from https://www.brainyquote.com/quotes/deborah_bull_241310?src=t_body_language

Carney, D. R., Cuddy, A. J. C., & Yap, A. J. (2010). Power posing: Brief nonverbal displays affect neuroendocrine levels and risk tolerance. *Psychological Science, 21*(10), 1363–1368. https://doi.org/10.1177/0956797610383437

Changing Minds. (n.d.). *Lips body language*. Changingminds.org. http://changingminds.org/techniques/body/parts_body_language/lips_body_language.htm

Christensen, T. (2023a, January 5). *What is body language? (with pictures)*. Language Humanities. https://www.languagehumanities.org/what-is-body-language.htm

Christensen, T. (2023b, January 28). *What is thin-slicing? (with picture)*. Language Humanities. https://www.languagehumanities.org/what-is-thin-slicing.htm

Cuddy, A. (n.d.). *Amy Cuddy quotes*. BrainyQuote. Retrieved February 20, 2023, from https://www.brainyquote.com/quotes/amy_cuddy_864904

de Groot, J. H. B., Kirk, P. A., & Gottfried, J. A. (2020). Encoding fear intensity in human sweat. *Philosophical Transactions of the Royal Society B: Biological Sciences, 375*(1800), 20190271. https://doi.org/10.1098/rstb.2019.0271

Dhikav, V., & Anand, K. S. (2012). Hippocampus in health and disease: An overview. *Annals of Indian Academy of Neurology, 15*(4), 239. https://doi.org/10.4103/0972-2327.104323

Discover the body language of the arms (get a grip). (2021, August 7). Body Language Matters. https://bodylanguagematters.com/discover-the-body-language-of-the-arms/

Dosanjh, D. (n.d.). *Diljit Dosanjh quotes.* BrainyQuote. Retrieved February 24, 2023, from https://www.brainyquote.com/quotes/diljit_dosanjh_1105613?src=t_body_language

Durante, K. M., Li, N. P., & Haselton, M. G. (2008). Changes in women's choice of dress across the ovulatory cycle: Naturalistic and laboratory task-based evidence. *Personality and Social Psychology Bulletin, 34*(11), 1451–1460. https://doi.org/10.1177/0146167208323103

Edelstein, L. G. (2022, November 22). *Decoding body language: 9 clear signs that someone is lying | Meetings & Conventions.* Www.meetings-Conventions.com. https://www.meetings-conventions.com/News/Third-Party/Body-Language-Signs-Someone-Is-Lying

Edwards, V. V. (2019, March 6). *20 hand gestures you should be using.* Medium. https://medium.com/@vvanedwards/20-hand-gestures-you-should-be-using-c8717eca02d7

Edwards, V. V. (2021a, January 6). *Feet behavior–The untapped body language you should know.* Science of People. https://www.scienceofpeople.com/feet-body-language/

Edwards, V. V. (2021b, March 9). *13 hidden nonverbal cues you should know: Neck body language.* Science of People. https://www.scienceofpeople.com/neck-body-language/#_ftn2

Edwards, V. V. (2021c, March 9). *How to get someone to open up using 20 body language cues.* Science of People. https://www.scienceofpeople.com/torso-body-language/#_ftn2

Edwards, V. V. (2021d, March 16). *60 hand gestures you should be using and their meaning.* Science of People. https://www.scienceofpeople.com/hand-gestures/#20-hand-gestures-you-should-be-using-and-their-meaning

Edwards, V. V. (2021e, March 20). *26 head body language gestures to get you a-head of the game.* Science of People. https://www.scienceofpeople.com/head-body-language/#_ftn4

Edwards, V. V. (2021f, April 2). *10 shoulder body language cues to help you read minds.* Science of People. https://www.scienceofpeople.com/shoulder-body-language/

Edwards, V. V. (2021g, April 21). *15 nose body language cues (rubbing, touching, and more!).* Science of People. https://www.scienceofpeople.com/nose-body-language/

Ekman, P. (2018, September 25). *Why do people lie: 9 motives for telling lies.* Paul Ekman Group. https://www.paulekman.com/blog/why-do-people-lie-motives/

Fasoli, F., Maass, A., Volpato, C., & Pacilli, M. G. (2018). The (female) graduate: Choice and consequences of women's clothing. *Frontiers in Psychology*, *9*. https://doi.org/10.3389/fpsyg.2018.02401

Goldin-Meadow, S. (2014). How gesture works to change our minds. *Trends in Neuroscience and Education*, *3*(1), 4–6. https://doi.org/10.1016/j.tine.2014.01.002

Goman, C. K. (2018, August 26). *5 ways body language impacts leadership results*. Forbes. https://www.forbes.com/sites/carolkinseygoman/2018/08/26/5-ways-body-language-impacts-leadership-results/?sh=2f876a49536a

Guber, P. (n.d.). *Peter Guber quotes*. BrainyQuote. Retrieved February 8, 2023, from https://www.brainyquote.com/quotes/peter_guber_503229?src=t_body_language

Hart, K. (n.d.). *A quote by Kevin Hart*. Www.goodreads.com. Retrieved February 17, 2023, from https://www.goodreads.com/quotes/9321131-it-s-spoken-with-a-shoulder-shrug-a-side-to-side-of-the

Holland, T. (2018, April 28). *Dignity health | facts about touch*. www.dignity-health.org. https://www.dignityhealth.org/articles/facts-about-touch-how-human-contact-affects-your-health-and-relationships

Howland, R. H. (2014). Vagus nerve stimulation. *Current Behavioral Neuroscience Reports*, *1*(2), 64–73. https://doi.org/10.1007/s40473-014-0010-5

https://www.facebook.com/verywell. (2019). *5 tips to better understand facial expressions*. Verywell Mind. https://www.verywellmind.com/understanding-emotions-through-facial-expressions-3024851

Hupp, S. (2021, March 9). *What does the hands on hips pose mean? 10 hip cues to know*. Science of People. https://www.scienceofpeople.com/hip-body-language/

Hutmacher, F. (2019). Why is there so much more research on vision than on any other sensory modality? *Frontiers in psychology*, *10*(2246). https://doi.org/10.3389/fpsyg.2019.02246

Iliades, C. (2010, July 14). *The truth about lies*. EverydayHealth.com. https://www.everydayhealth.com/longevity/truth-about-lies-and-longevity.aspx

Leg Posture, B. L. (2020). *Body language—leg posture reveals our mind's intent*. Westsidetoastmasters.com. https://westsidetoastmasters.com/resources/book_of_body_language/chap10.html

McCarty, K., Darwin, H., Cornelissen, P. L., Saxton, T. K., Tovée, M. J., Caplan, N., & Neave, N. (2017). Optimal asymmetry and other motion parameters that characterize high-quality female dance. *Scientific Reports*, *7*(1). https://doi.org/10.1038/srep42435

Mehrabian, A., & Ferris, S. R. (1967). Inference of attitudes from nonverbal communication in two channels. *Journal of Consulting Psychology*, *31*(3),

248–252. https://doi.org/10.1037/h0024648

Miller, J. K., Westerman, D. L., & Lloyd, M. E. (2004). Are first impressions lasting impressions? An exploration of the generality of the primacy effect in memory for repetitions. *Memory & Cognition, 32*(8), 1305–1315. https://doi.org/10.3758/bf03206321

ModernGov, U. (2020). *Why is body language important in communication?* Blog.moderngov.com. https://blog.moderngov.com/why-is-body-language-important-in-communication

Ora, H., Wada, M., Salat, D., & Kansaku, K. (2016). Arm crossing updates brain functional connectivity of the left posterior parietal cortex. *Scientific Reports, 6*(1). https://doi.org/10.1038/srep28105

Petruzzi, J. (2019, October 9). *Observing body language- thin-slicing-and behavioral profiling.* Www.linkedin.com. https://www.linkedin.com/pulse/observing-body-language-thin-slicing-and-behavioural-jimmy-petruzzi

Pouga, L., Berthoz, S., de Gelder, B., & Grèzes, J. (2010). Individual differences in socio affective skills influence the neural bases of fear processing: The case of alexithymia. *Human Brain Mapping, 31*(10), 1469–1481. https://doi.org/10.1002/hbm.20953

Rothfuss, P. (2011). *Truth and lies quotes (96 quotes).* Goodreads.com. https://www.goodreads.com/quotes/tag/truth-and-lies